The Origin of the Prolonged Economic Stagnation in Contemporary Japan

The deflationary Japanese economy is a spurious observation and a precarious political propaganda, which tacitly connects with the fanatic diagnosis urging an inflation-prompting macroeconomic policy.

This book provides an overview of the prolonged stagnation of the current Japanese economy. It also examines the politico-economic implications concerning the precarious conversion of Japanese monetary policy, and it focuses on the vulnerability of the price-sustaining policy concerning the public debt. The book also analyzes and suggests against the acceleration of inflation under the current Japanese foreign exchange system, and proposes that the surge of foreign direct investment towards East Asia is the acute cause of Japanese economic stagnation.

The book concludes that in order to rebuild the economic potential of the Japanese economy, it is essential to educate and foster youths. This book will definitely interest those who are keen to learn more about the relationship between the Bank of Japan and the Japanese political parties.

Masayuki Otaki is Professor at the Institute of Social Sciences, the University of Tokyo. He received his PhD in Economics from the University of Tokyo, and his research interests are macroeconomic theory and environmental economics.

The Origin of the Prolonged Economic Stagnation in Contemporary Japan

The factitious deflation and meltdown of the Japanese firm as an entity

Masayuki Otaki

Routledge
Taylor & Francis Group
LONDON AND NEW YORK

First published 2016 by Routledge

2 Park Square, Milton Park, Abingdon, Oxfordshire OX14 4RN

711 Third Avenue, New York, NY 10017

Routledge is an imprint of the Taylor & Francis Group, an informa business

First issued in hardback 2018

British Library Cataloguing-in-Publication Data
A catalogue record for this book is available from the British Library

Library of Congress Cataloging-in-Publication Data
Otaki, Masayuki, 1957– The origin of the prolonged economic stagnation in
   contemporary Japan / Masayuki Otaki.
      pages cm
  1. Japan—Economic conditions—1945– 2. Japan—Economic policy—
1945– 3. Stagnation (Economics) 4. Deflation (Finance)—Japan.
5. Industries—Japan—History. I. Title.
   HC462.95.O836 2015
   330.952—dc23
   2015011855

ISBN: 978-0-415-73444-8 (hbk)
ISBN: 978-1-138-31696-6 (pbk)

Typeset in Times New Roman
by Apex CoVantage, LLC

Contents

PART IV
Towards the reincarnation of Japanese economy 107

Figures

Tables

Preface

Edmund Burke, whose book *Reflections on the Revolution in France* is one of Keynes' favorite books, was an extremely liberal politician. However, according to Norman (2013), he should be classified among conservatives. Norman defines conservative individuals as (1) those who put much importance on what history tells us, and taking changes in historical environments into consideration, consider the necessities of political-economic reformation incessantly; and (2) those who negate radicalism such as revolution because its substance is an internal war that adjoins violence, and believe in gradualism presuming that human beings are a creature that is apt to be erroneous.

As long as such a definition is persuasive, my economic thought also belongs to being conservative. Although this book is a critical analysis of the current Japanese economy, it never means that I defy some kind of efficiency that market mechanism possibly achieves. Conversely, what this book articulates is how to bring into harmony the potentials of market mechanism with the strained political situations in Japan.

If we regard a stringent planning economy as a kind of radicalism, as Burke grievously criticizes, it is by no means limited to communism and socialism. The precarious right-wings in Japan between the World War I and II were also hard social planners in reality. Thus, conservativeness is an indispensable and critical political thought for keeping a democratic economy from despotism.

Since the beginning of this century, the Japanese government has alleged that in order to recover the Japanese economy, it is urgent to work on privatization, deregulation and globalization. Such a political talk seems that the Japanese government is eager to establish the market discipline because many out-of-date regulations hinder the economic growth and stagnate the economy.

Nevertheless, in reality, these seemingly market-friendly policies, summarized by the name of the Structural Reformation (Kozo Kaikaku), are a kind of vicious social planning that aims to protect the vested interests of wealthy strata. In this sense, democracy and sound market economy in Japan face a grievous crisis. Since the true aims of the Structural Reformation are disguised by the intensive and commercially poisoned propaganda issued by irresponsible mass media, citizens, who are lay in economics, tend to blindly believe the government's propaganda.

As a typical type of these spurious market-friendly policies, one can find continual revisions of the law of non-tenured employees (The Worker Dispatching Act: WDA; Rodosha Haken Ho) under the Koizumi cabinets that coincides with the surge of foreign direct investment (FDI). These revisions nominally advocate that high wage payments to tenured employees lessens the competitiveness of Japan when compared to East Asian economies especially Chinese economy, and hence the deregulation of the Japanese labor markets, which implies substantial wage reductions and the aggravation of employment conditions such as social securities, is acutely required.

It should be noted that the relatively high wages in Japan can be attributed much to the very existence of non-tradable goods such as housing service rather than employees' self-interested behavior, because most population of Japan concentrates within narrow urban areas. Accordingly, Japanese employees are not affluent as they look. Meanwhile, market mechanism, ipso fact, is not important; it should be a supreme existence only because it enhances an economy's well-being *as a whole*. This is the most important message of this book. Thus, revisions of WDA, which permits to import large amount of unskilled and cheap foreign labor force and/or promotes the surge of FDI, is apparently undesirable for Japanese employees, although it is beneficial for the small groups of affluent employer and/or stockholder.

As this example suggests, applications of naïve laissez-faire policy to an economy are quite precarious as much as a stringent social planning. It should be emphasized that market possibly fails to achieve efficient allocation as social planning in socialist countries has. In other words, people living in a market economy are apt to be unaware of the egregious fact that market mechanism can be manipulated in favor of very small affluent groups. That is, one must note that government failures are possibly aggravated by the contraction of a government. What is acutely important is whether a government is well-disciplined not only by market but also by citizens as a whole.

This discussion implies that there are important and prerequisite regulations for hindering a market economy from becoming dysfunctional. Most of this book critically examines whether such regulations are properly managed in the current Japanese economy. It also provides diagnoses for achieving stable efficient resource allocation and fair income distribution under a stationary economy negating the imperativeness of economic growth.

Part I

The politico-economic situation in contemporary Japan

1 An overview of the prolonged stagnation era

The 'Structural Reformation' that made matters worse

1.1 The rift between theory and reality of the market economy: the metamorphose of laissez-faire scheme from social cohesion to social Darwinism

Many economists optimistically believe that any sort of competition heightens the economic efficiency. However, we must note that *efficiency* cannot be defined without its objectives. That is, efficiency means a measure which attains a given objective at the minimal cost. Therefore, whenever we discuss whether some policy heightens efficiency, we must clarify what is the ultimate aim of such a policy and whether the aim is relevant for the national economy's well-being.

The authentic theory of laissez-faire is an ideal theory of social cohesion. Generally, economics evaluates the efficacy of an economy from the viewpoint of Pareto efficiency. Pareto efficiency is a moderate social coherent value judgment. It is defined as a situation where at least one individual becomes disadvantageous whenever an individual strives to be more advantageous. Thus, if the market economy is Pareto efficient, it is apparent that no one is impoverished by the competition if the incomes are properly redistributed.

Thus, the concept of Pareto efficiency implies that cruel cutthroat competitions, which deprive of the breathing space for one's everyday life, would never occur. This is partly because the equal opportunities of politico-economy are guaranteed to all individuals, and also because the property rights of every individual are thought to exist without any unreasonable governmental intervention. Moreover, prices are assumed to be public facilities, which no particular individual can manipulate for his or her own economic interests. Thus, under such an ideal circumstance of the market economy, every individual can freely economize his or her possessions for achieving the maximum utility.

Accordingly, such a system never incurs any kind of cutthroat competition which invades the breathing space of its counterparts. The laissez-faire theory (The First Fundament Theory of Welfare Economics) establishes the ideal conditions necessary for the market economy to achieve the Pareto efficiency. In this sense, the theory of laissez-faire provides prerequisites for the sound working of the market economy.

As mentioned before, the laissez-faire theory as a social cohesion is deeply rooted in the respect for property rights and the equality of politico-economic opportunities. Every individual seeks the maximal utilization under the budget constraint. In other words, this means that he or she strives to minimize his or her expenditure for attaining a given utilization level. That is, the deed, which everyone selfishly pursues for his or her own economic well-being, unconsciously leads the society to economize scarce resources as a whole. Since such an economic motive is derived from the fact that the individual scarifies his or her own resources for his or her economic well-being, the guarantee that there will be no intrusion of private property is crucial for the market economy. In other words, whenever such a basic principle is violated, the laissez-fair scheme ceases to be a social cohesion theory.

This, in turn, implies that once private property rights are trespassed by political (via direct enforcement) or monopoly power (via indirect prices/wages manipulation) and the economizing discipline is slacked, the scarce resources are socially wasted by the prerogative strata. We find a typical example of such social waste in the young generation's labor markets in contemporary Japan. Japanese juveniles compete not only with each other, but also, potentially, with the abundant and cheaper labor forces in the East Asia economies. In this sense, the Japanese firms possess the monopsony power on the domestic labor market and are able to cut wages and force the high-working intensities. Theoretically, this means that leisure (one of the scarce resources belonging to each private property) is abused by the prerogative which allows the wage manipulation.

We must also note that almost all Japanese young individuals do not have the opportunities to voice and join the personal and management decisions within firms. Such lack of the opportunities is the overt source of the prerogative on which elder generations decisively rely.

Most uncultivated businessmen advocate that various skills are required for the young generation to survive the international competition. Indeed, they even do not hesitate to declare that only 'high-skilled' youths can survive. However, it is unclear what those skills imply, and such an advocacy is mainly used as a measure for eliminating working opportunities and lowering wages of young individuals. As a result, the labor markets for the youth are under cutthroat competition. They are forced to search for their jobs and work under quite disadvantageous circumstances.

As such, once the exempt from the intrusion of private property rights and/or the equal politico-economic opportunities is publicly endorsed, the laissez-faire scheme transforms from the social cohesion theory to the ominous social Darwinism, which was the notorious theoretical pillar of the totalitarianism. This chapter considers the reasons why such an appalling politico-economic situation is generated during the prolonged stagnation after the Bubble Economy in the second half of the 1980s.

1.2   The origin of despotic capitalism: for or whom is the laissez-faire scheme?

In general, there is no discontinuity in history. If one consummately examines historical facts, he or she will surely find that the seeds, which prescribe the current economic conditions, have been sown beforehand. The seemingly sudden and drastic changes in history owe much to careless observations and/or thoughts of historians and/or economists.

In this sense, we need to explore the characteristics of the Bubble Economy (the second half of the 1980s) and compare them with those in the prolonged stagnation era. It is our basic understanding that the prominent characteristics of the prolonged stagnation era, which we shall name the *despotic capitalism*, were already prepared and formed within the Bubble Economy and are being strengthened throughout the prolonged stagnation era.

As discussed above, it is necessary for the sound operation of market economy to establish two main principles. One is the prohibition of intrusion of private properties. The other is warranting the equal opportunity to every kind of politico-economic activity. We define despotic capitalism as a market economy where one or both of the conditions above are not satisfied.

Under the despotic capitalism, the laissez-faire scheme does not mean that the politico-economic activity of everyone is at their discretion as the standard economics tells us. Instead, it implies that those who have the prerogatives to trespass the private property right and/or others' opportunities for politico-economic activities substantively become exempted not only from the legal persecution but also from the criticism from the viewpoint of the social norm of the market economy.

Indeed, such vicious deeds, which will ultimately paralyze functions of the market economy, are mistakenly considered to be the deeds of those who are winners or heroes in the cutthroat competition and who built huge fortunes. This tendency is exacerbated by the information manipulation of the mass media. As such, the despotic capitalism is far from the social coherent market economy, which standard economics presupposes. The laissez-faire principle is not applied equally to every resident, but is confined to a very limited number of people who enjoy their prerogatives.

1.2.1 Pseudo laissez-faire for wealthy strata: lessons from the monetary policy during the Bubble Economy

As precisely analyzed below, the 'Structural Reformation' (Kozo Kaikaku) that originated from the Koizumi cabinet is characterized by two distinct features: privatization and deregulation. The logic which sustains these neoliberal policy schemes is quite simple. Whenever idling resources exist, the prices become lower and effectively of use, unless government unreasonably interferes with the market mechanism. The emancipation from such oppressive measures encourages active entrepreneurships, and thus the stagnant economy is reincarnated.

However, such a crude proposition is not always upheld. For an acute example, let us look back on the prestagnation era, namely, the era of the Bubble Economy (the second half of the 1980s), specifically concerning the monetary policy of the Bank of Japan (BOJ).

Throughout this era, despite stock and land prices hike, the BOJ continued accommodating the explosively increasing demand for money without sufficient precaution, which was required for stimulating further speculation. That is, the

BOJ adopted the *pseudo laissez-faire* monetary policy, which almost entirely submits to wills of the private financial institutions and is far from preventing the excessive speculation.

There are two main reasons why the BOJ took such a speculation-friendly policy. One is that the Consumer Price Index (CPI) had been stable and that the burst of asset prices was not their concern because The Law of the Bank of Japan (Nihon Ginko Ho) prescribed that the highest priority of the monetary policy was stabilizing the price level.[1]

The other is the precaution that a hike in the short-term interest squeezes the profits out of the financial institutions and is harmful for their business environment (Okina 1993). This is a pervasive statement concerning the pseudo laissez-faire monetary policy during zealous speculative economic situations.

Consider that once the private financial institutions weave such an accommodative stance of the monetary authority to avoid an abrupt increase in the short-term interest, they advance their speculative positions because no additional interest cost is expected to be incurred, and thus, they are completely free from the fear of the bust of asset prices. This is a kind of moral-hazard behavior due to the improper laissez-faire monetary policy in the era dominated by enthusiastic speculation.

One may argue that if the regulations concerning the ratio of land-relating assets to the total assets by the Ministry of Finance (MOF) were indefinitely postponed, the asset prices could maintain the exorbitant level. However, such an argument evidently neglects the very existence of the fundamental values.

Although it is difficult to calculate the exact fundamental value of assets, everyone scarcely denies that there is an upper-limit price that he or she can afford to buy his or her residence. Let us show how the fundamental value is calculated although it is a round number. Suppose that the annual income of a standard Japanese individual is 6 million yens (a little more income than actual) and that the interest rate of housing loan is 0.05 (a little less than the rate during the Bubble Economy). In addition, the individual repays the loan in 30 years. Finally, his or her gross average propensity of saving is 0.3 (rather higher than actual).

Then the upper limit price of this residence q is

$$q = 0.3 \times 6 \times \left[1 + \frac{1}{1.05} + \frac{1}{[1.05]^2} + \cdots + \frac{1}{[1 + 0.05]^{30-1}} \right] \approx 0.3 \times 6 \times 21 = 37.8$$

(millions yen)

Thus, the fundamental value of the residence is about six times the income. In addition, we must note that more will be deducted from savings because household's savings will, in addition to repayment, cover other costs (e.g., private pension funds, educational costs for children). Hence, as suggested by the assumptions above, this price is rather overestimated.

Prime Minister Kiichi Miyazawa once alleged that one of the economic goals of his cabinet was to ensure that people would be able to purchase their residence at the expense that is five times their annual income (The New Fundamental Life Standard Law [Shin Seikatsu Kihon Ho] 1992). Such an assertion suggests that our estimation is not far from the fundamental price (i.e., the upper-limit price of a residence at which a standard citizen can purchase).

Furthermore, the price index of residence (Tosho Jutaku Shisu) fell about 40 per cent during these two decades, and astonishingly, it still costs about 35 million yen to purchase a condominium not smaller than 60 m² nearby Tokyo Metropolitan area, even 20 years after the bust of the Bubble.

In conjunction with the above estimation, such evidence suggest that the price of a residence was overvalued by about 40 per cent at the peak of the Bubble Economy and that the price of a residence diverges far from its fundamental value.

We must note that the fundamental price of an asset is the bottom price within the speculative market. Although the market price may soar far beyond the fundamental price at least temporally, the speculation never succeeds unless the investor can find his or her trading counterpart.

Because the residence market mostly includes ordinary citizens whose income is under 6 million yens and who are thus not able to pay the debt, the speculative bubble cannot expand or even sustain itself whenever the bit price of the market requires some large margin on its fundamental value. The speculative investors are ultimately unable to find their transaction counterparts, thereby the Bubble busting.

We should not overlook the fact that the gains and losses from the speculation are two side of the same coin. That is, the process of a speculative bubble is that of the income transfer from losers to winners and genetically zero-sum game. For example, consider that some landlord earned 10 million yens by selling a part of his or her land, and his or her transaction counterpart lose the same amount of the money due to the collapse of the speculative bubble. It immediately implies that 10 million yens are transferred from the unwise speculator to the landlord.

In the short run, the capital losses are not easily actualized because the direction to which land prices move is obscure, and the capital gain earned by landlords stimulates their consumption and temporally upturns the business condition. This is the mechanism by which speculative bubbles coincide with a boom.

However, sooner or later, the bubble busts via the aforementioned process, and the huge capital losses are realized. Henceforth, this severely shrinks economic activities. That is, Japanese economy during the Bubble Era surely flourished in exchange for the unforeseen future huge cost of bulk of non-performing debts.

Accordingly, if the regulations on land and residence were much delayed, the damage of the Japanese economy from the bust of the Bubble Economy would have been exorbitant. In other words, although many economists consider that the curtailment of the reduction or deduction of non-performing debts paralyzed the Japanese economy afterwards (they vaguely call this era the 'Lost Decade' or 'Lost Two Decades'), such an assertion is not necessarily a proper diagnosis. The vital cause of the seemingly prolonged stagnation is the pseudo laissez-faire and money market friendly monetary policy adopted by the BOJ.

This exemplifies serious evidence which suggests that some regulatory measures are unavoidable to achieve the excellent social cohesion in the market economy, specifically for managing public goods such as money and credit. A ruthless application of the laissez-faire measure to these social substances is prone to harm the social cohesion as the example of the accommodative monetary policy suggests. Such a pseudo laissez-faire measure provided wealthy strata, which have enough money to access the land and/or stock market trading, for spurious benefits before the bust of the Bubble. Consequently, the money lost by unwise speculators was partly financed by unrelated standard citizens via huge issues of public debts, which ultimately become tax burdens. This is an acute roundabout trespass to the private property rights.

1.2.2   Does the pseudo laissez-faire scheme always imply privatization? Evidence from The New Bank Tokyo (Shin Ginko Tokyo)

As sketched in Section 1.2.1, the main pillar, which supports the pseudo laissez-fair policies, is the efficiency of the private sector relative to the public sector. Since the private sector is incentivized by earning profits as much as possible, it can economize unnecessary resources. In contrast with such a high efficiency in the private sector, the public sector cannot be disciplined by the threat of the bankruptcy, and thus many resources are poured into wasteful objects.

As such, economists, who eagerly support the pseudo laissez-fair policies, assert that the privatization of the public sector should be advanced via deregulation. It is natural that most laypeople in economics believe that deregulation aims to heighten the efficiency of Japanese economy via privatization of the public sector, thereby promising business upturn.

However, there are many examples including 'the Third Sectors' (Daisan Sekuta), which exhibit that the assertion of privatization is illusory and that the laissez-fair scheme is maneuvered quite arbitrarily. The following is the most prominent example.

The example is the establishment of The New Bank Tokyo (Shin Ginko Tokyo). The New Bank Tokyo was established in April 2004 by the strong initiative of Shintaro Ishihara who was the governor of Tokyo Metropolitan in charge. The bank was established through the direct acquisition of the private bank (the BNB Bariba Trust Bank) by Tokyo Metropolitan.

Although Ishihara's prospects concerning Tokyo Metropolitan and Japanese economy as a whole are rather vague, and it is an exaggeration to regard him as a simple laissez-faire believer (he is one of famous dissidents to TPP), the fact that the gigantic public sector absorbs the private bank and the monetary authority also permitted such a provocative deed is quite important. One must note that this acquisition was settled just when The Minster of State of Financial Services in charge was Heizo Takenaka in the first Koizumi cabinet, and he is the most prominent advocate of pseudo laissez-faire policy.

The New Bank Tokyo was established for rescuing small- and medium-size non-financial firms, which are said to be often forced to face financial distresses. The bank aims to mitigate such difficulties and makes firms resilient. However, there were many private incumbents within such a market: the local banks (Chiho Ginko), the second local banks (Daini Chiho Ginko), the credit banks (Shinyo Kinko), and the credit unions (Shinyo Kumiai).

It is apparent that not only the above banks, but also other types of banks are against such an inconsistent public policy. The New Bank Tokyo was excluded from the Japanese Bankers Association (Zenkoku Ginko Kyokai) from its beginning.

Since incumbent banks had already established the intimate customer relationship to the targeted firms by the New Bank Tokyo, this bank has never achieved good performance. The cumulative deficit from 2007 to 2013 was approximately 78 billion yens. This exceeds its own capital by about four times. There is scarce hope that such a heavily indebted bank can be sustainable without some unfavorable public interventions.[2]

What is more precarious is the fact the New Bank Tokyo still continues offering exorbitant high deposit rates despite the messy business conditions. This bank offers 0.3 per cent interest against one-year deposit less than 10 million yens, which exceeds Mizuho Bank's (the biggest private bank in Japan) offer rate against the same class of deposit by more than 10 times (the rates in August 2013). Furthermore, this bank offers far lower rate against the deposit over 10 million yens. This is counterintuitive considering other banks' offers. We must herewith note that the upper limit of the deposit which is covered by the Deposit Insurance Corporation of Japan (Yokin Hoken Kiko) is 10 million yen.

This is a typical moral hazard owing to the limited liability. Even though this bank goes to bankrupt and pay off, the deposit insurance exempts this bank from the redemption of the small unit deposit, and thus there is no substantive cost for collecting such kind of deposit. This bank free-rides the deposit insurance system and tries to finance its hoarding huge non-performing debts. If such an unfavorable and irresponsible deed prevails among financial institutions, which face the business crises, the deposit insurance system becomes unsustainable as a whole, and the stability of financial market is heavily injured.

To summarize, the pseudo laissez-faire does not necessary imply the privatization and never contributes to the national well-being. This is a typical example of the unrestricted dissipation which is allowed for the prerogative strata. In this sense, the required consistencies between laws are slacked, and the principle of the governance by law is paralyzed from the beginning of the Structural Reformation by the Koizumi cabinet.

1.2.3 The aggravation of the disparity of economic opportunities: the economic consequence of exorbitant foreign direct investment and the deregulation of the domestic labor market

As it was mentioned above, a market economy is unable to contribute to the nation's well-being whenever the equal economic opportunity is not ensured because the fair competition, which is necessary for achieving the efficient resource allocation, became dysfunctional. Most current Japanese college students are disillusioned on their appalling future. They are forced to work under cheap wages and more vulnerable employment environment (liable to be fired) compared with those until the 1990s. It is well-known that many Japanese could enjoy the 'long-term employment convention' (Shushin Koyo Sei), which implies that his or her job is almost secured within a firm for a long duration and is scarcely fired excluding the exceptional case.

As briefly discussed in Section 1.1, such a tragic and downturn circumstance as surrounding the numerous Japanese youths of potential ability never stems from the harsh competition within them. It is one of the inevitable economic consequences of the exorbitant foreign direct investment (FDI) especially towards East Asia, where low-wage labor forces are abundant. The surge of FDI, which becomes prominent from the Koizumi cabinet (see Figure 1.1),[3] exports the real capital and employment opportunities, and instead, it imports unrealizable and spurious profits,[4] and mass unemployment.

The imported unemployment especially aggravates the new entrants' job markets, which mostly comprise the Japanese youths (see Table 1.1).

To stimulate further FDI, the subsequent cabinets since Koizumi's advance deregulations concerning the Labor Law (Rodo Ho), which prescribes working conditions to prevent the abuse of monopsony of employees in the labor market. Although the process seems rather complicated, the goal of such deregulations is apparent. First, it is necessary for promoting FDI to shutter incumbent domestic factories and offices instead of building up new alternatives in East Asia. Accordingly, regulations for the preventing employees from the abuse of the right of fire of employers should be gradually abolished.

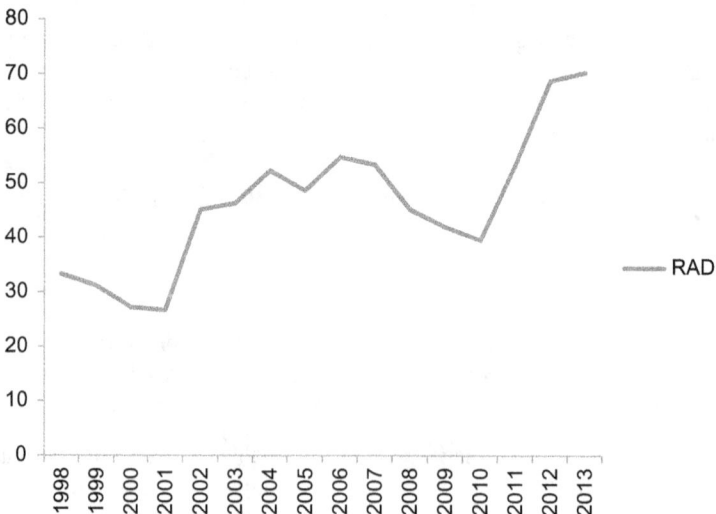

Figure 1.1 The surge of FDI in Japan

Table 1.1 The unemployment rate in Japan (Classified by Age)

Year\Age	15–24	25–34	35–44	45–54	55–64
2007	7.7	4.9	3.4	2.8	3.4
2008	7.2	5.2	3.4	2.9	3.6
2009	9.1	6.4	4.6	3.9	4.7
2010	9.4	6.2	4.6	3.9	5.0
2011	8.2	5.7	4.2	3.5	4.4
2012	8.3	5.5	4.1	3.3	4.1

Data Source: Labor Force Survey (Ministry of Internal Affairs and Communications, Statistic Bureau).

Second, the bargaining power of employees prominently wanes via such deregulations in conjunction with the flux of FDI. Many employees are deprived of their tenures and forced to bear wage-cutting and unstable employment environment. An employee under 20 experienced about 15 per cent wage cut during the 2000s. An employee 20 to 24 years old had about 10 per cent wage cut during the same period (Survey on Wage Structure of Private Sectors by National Tax Agency [Minikan Kyuyo Jittai Chosa]).

Both effects of the deregulations in the labor market are apparently advantageous to employers because these deregulations extend the one-sided opportunities for employers to access new markets. Conversely, the employees are forced to face appalling conditions because most of them lose opportunities to access favorable labor market conditions.

A muzzy neoclassical economist might argue that if the youths who are deprived of domestic employment opportunities access the capital market and purchase profitable stocks of FDI firms and/or establish their own firm that ruthlessly relies on the lower-wage labor forces in East Asia, then, no matter how small his or her firm is, the equal opportunity to market competition is ensured even in a flux of FDI and its adjacent deregulations in labor markets.

Nevertheless, such argument is spurious and far from reality because the capital market is one of the most difficult markets for those who do not possess sufficient wealth.[5] Besides the substantive difficulties in nurturing management skills, the informational asymmetry on the capital investment is genetically prevalent between lenders (financial intermediaries) and borrowers (youths in this example). In addition, a debt contract presumes the limited liability, which implies that a borrower is emancipated from the fear of his or her nemesis. Hence, those who find much necessity in financing his or her enterprise are unable to obtain the lenders' credits and are excluded from the capital market.

Moreover, the above discussion neglects the huge business risk relative to the wealth which the standard citizen possesses. Whenever we take the business risk into account, the matter becomes worse. Once the business fails and he or she bankrupts, this becomes the fatal or incurable wound for his or her life and the life of his or her family. The business risk is far severe compared with the risk of frictional unemployment, from which the individual can recover by finding a new job. As such, the structural unemployment caused by FDI deprives many standard citizens of the opportunities of stable economic life.

Thus, the serious increase in the unemployment adjacent to FDI is an impasse for the equal economic opportunity of standard citizens who are not wealthy enough to access the capital market and bear various business risks. On the other hand, FDI ensues more profitable opportunities for the wealthy strata, although it is precarious as discussed in Chapters 5 and 6. As such, the disparity of the accessible economic opportunities has been substantively exacerbated by the surge of FDI and the deregulation of the labor market. This is also an overt onus of the despotic capitalism.

1.3   The crisis of the Japanese market economy and democracy: the pseudo laissez-faire scheme is a roundabout trespass on private property rights

What do the above three contradictive examples mean? At least, we find that the pseudo laissez-faire policy scheme does not necessarily mean the one-sided privatization, and furthermore, the pseudo laissez-faire policy scheme, the assertion of which the Structural Reformation (Kozo Kaikaku) relies on, aims not to provide more equal economic freedom, but the economic despotism shared by the prerogative strata.

If we once accept such a view, there is no wonder about the implications of the above seemingly contradictive economic policies. As far as, some policy measures are beneficial for a prerogative stratum, the profit or rent seeking is recommendable, and such deeds are permitted and prompted under the name of laissez-faire without conferring to the economic welfare of Japanese economy as a whole.

This is an acute crisis of the Japanese market economy. The sound working of a market economy, which unequivocally means the efficacy of the market economy, basically depends on the two presumptions mentioned above. The first is the right to exempt from the intrusion of private property. The second is the potential equal opportunity of all transaction. The pseudo laissez-faire scheme entirely contradicts with these basic presumptions for a democratic and efficient market economy.

As Carr (1979) concisely depicted, the Russian Revolution specifically intruded the property rights of peasants. Owing to such ignorant and violent oppression, the agricultural sector had stagnated for more than 20 years thereafter. Not by so much crude and naïve as the Russian communist party, but via more roundabout way, the Japanese government tacitly intrudes property rights of citizens almost without hesitation.

The intrusion to property rights is unleashed via the following two ways. One is the huge accumulation of the public debt. It is certain to some extent that the citizens underestimate the true cost of the public investment and that this enlarges the budgetary deficit. However, we must note that the enormous non-performing private debts emerging from the bust of the Bubble mainly triggered the explosive public debt accumulation (see Table 1.2).

Table 1.2 Averaged increase ratio of public debt per annum (%)

Year	1981–1990	1990–1999	1999–2008	2008–2011
Ratio	0.2	12	4.7	4.0

Data Source: SNA Statistics (Cabinet Office).

To support such non-performing debts and rescue the banks, much public funds were poured, which are mainly financed by the deficit national debts (Akaji Kokusai). Since, as discussed in Section 1.2.1, the speculation is basically a zero-sum game, it is fair to levy the stratum which made huge amount of money during the Bubble Era.

The public debt, estimating from the current stock level, should be at least partially redeemed, while we should not excessively rely on the conversion to pre-serve the international credibility of the public debts. This surely incurs the additional taxation to citizens who are apparently unrelated to the bust of the Bubble.

Thus, although it is a roundabout way, the property rights of most citizens are trespassed in order to cancel the burden of the beaten speculators by the bust who are entirely unknowable for them. The example in Section 1.2.2 also provides us with the more typical example how our private property is trespassed in due process.

The second way of the indirect trespass of the individual property rights has been already depicted in Section 1.2.3. The nurtured skills for business, that is, the accumulated human capitals are the vital assets for most individuals. Many Japanese employers become shortsighted, and they concentrate to earn as many profits as possible in exchange of the sacrifice of nurtured skills of employees despite the fact that the true driving force of a firm is the intangible and common owned human capital, as analyzed in Chapters 5 and 6 in more detail.

The flux of FDI obsoletes such precious skills via the ruthless copy and transplant to East Asian economies, and thereby unreasonably forcing lower wages to incumbent and skilled Japanese employees. We must wholeheartedly note that the concept of the private property is not confined to tangible capital assets and also should be extended to intangible human capitals although they are difficult to evaluate. From this viewpoint, it is evident that the flux of FDI is not only a deprivation of equal opportunity of economic activities, but also an acute trespass of private property.

To summarize, the most precarious symptom in the Japanese market economy is that most citizens believe that the government, which advocates the pseudo laissez-faire scheme, possesses fidelity to the market economy. Japanese economy faces the crisis tilting to the despotic capitalism quite alike the socialist economy.

The only difference between the despotic capitalism and socialism is its despots: the stockholders or the communist party. The despotic capitalism is far worse than the socialism in the sense that no standard citizen can identify who are the true stockholders, and hence, they are hardly able to find the efficacious way how to resist such despotism and abdicate its despots.

Finally, let us clarify the relationship between two key concepts: despotic capitalism and pseudo lasses-faire scheme.

Definitions

A. The despotic capitalism is an inefficient market economy characterized by the following two conditions:

 1 The trespasses to the private property rights independent of whether they are verifiable.
 2 The deprivations of equal economic opportunities which should be independent of one's wealth and social status.

B. The pseudo laissez-fair scheme corresponds to various policy measures to progress the despotic capitalism.

1.4   Why do most Japanese people support despotic capitalism?

1.4.1   Disordered influx of information necessitates despots

As discussed in 1.2.3, the aggravation of the Japanese labor market mainly stems from the exorbitant FDI. The increase in unemployment is concentrated within the younger generations (not more than 19 years old and from 20 to 24 years old: see Table 1.4)

However, the younger generations illusorily consider that they have better employment opportunities than actual. About more than one-third of male employees who are less than 19, and 20 per cent of male employees between the age of 20 and 24, quit their jobs (See Table 1.3). According to the Survey on

Table 1.3 Participation, quit and conversion rate (%) by age (male 2011)

Rates\Age	19	20–24	25–29	30–34	35–39	40–44	45–49	50–54	55–60	60–64
Participation Rate	78.6	34.5	15.4	10.6	7.8	7.2	6.9	5.7	6.4	12.4
Quit Rate		36.8	22.3	14.6	10.7	7.7	7.7	6.8	7.0	8.9	23.6
Conversion Rate		13.3	13.7	12.2	9.0	6.9	6.2	5.9	4.9	5.4	10.6

Data Source: Survey on Employment Trend (Ministry of Health, Labor and Welfare).

Table 1.4 Averaged unemployment rate (%) of 15–24 years old and total male

Year	15–24	Total
1990–1999	6.2	3.1
2000–2009	9.9	4.6
2010–2013	9.6	5.2

Data Source: Labor Force Survey (Ministry of Internal Affairs and Communications, Statistic Bureau).

Employment Trends (Ministry of Health, Labor and Welfare 2011), the probabilities of success in job conversion are about 13 per cent (both 19 years and 20- to 24-year-old males), and thus 64 (=1 − 13.3/36.8) per cent of 19 years old and 39 (1− 13.3/22.3) per cent 20 to 24 years old become unemployed once they decide the conversion.

There are two striking features in such a serious unemployment of the younger generations. One is that such unemployment will be prolonged and persistent, and that once a youth loses his job, it is quite difficult for him to recapture the chance. As depicted in Table 1.3, the inflow and the outflow equilibrate within the other senior generations (note that the conversion rate is almost able to explain the parallel movements of inflow and outflow of each generation). This proves that there is scarce room to cut in afterward for the youths if they lose their jobs.

The other feature is more striking. The motive of two-thirds of the youth who left their jobs is voluntary. The quittance owing to the expiry of the contract and dismissal by their employer is only a quarter (the Survey on Employment Trends). Despite such a hardship, why do youths leave their jobs so easily?

The disordered influx of information seriously affects such a rash behavior. Specifically, the Japanese mass media (including the employment-agency industry) are quite sinful. Despite the fact that the employment opportunities for the youths are extremely narrowed by the surge of FDI as a whole, they incessantly release various and momentary information concerning how the youths can succeed in getting good jobs, and many students innocently believe that such a convenient procedure really exists.

There are two prominent features of such kind of the influx of information: (1) the inconsistency contained in itself, and (2) the summoning of the unattainable enthusiasm that they can easily get a high-payment and stable jobs. The Japanese mass media propagate that any student can get a good job if he or she faithfully follows the method which they provide in return for the non-negligible charge.

Such an assertion evidently contains the inconsistency, because some parts of students are inevitably excluded beforehand owing to the macroeconomic conditions against the labor market. To avoid such inconsistency being revealed, the contents of so-called know-how for getting job, which is provided by job mediator companies, are incessantly and slightly changed year by year.

The job mediator companies exaggerate the benefit of the job conversion. Based on the Survey on Employment Trends, we can estimate the success probability of the job conversion of the Japanese youths, although it is a round number. About three-quarters of youths under 19 can succeed in entering a firm (2011). ~~Fourteen~~ Thirteen per cent of them change their jobs, and only a quarter of the job-converging youths become able to earn income 10 per cent higher than previous one. These numbers imply that a new entrant into high teenagers market can success via job conversion with the probability

$$(0.13/0.75) \times 0.25 = 0.04$$

That is, the success via job conversion is quite difficult in reality (with the probability of only 4 per cent).

Furthermore, as discussed above, we must note that the labor markets for the seniors are almost closed (see Table 1.3) and that there are scarce chances to get the job once they cannot find or lose their jobs when they are young.

To summarize, the Japanese labor market for the youths is characterized by the following two undeniable facts. First, the youths are in turbulence caused by the factitious advertisement of the mass media, including employment agencies. They are incautious about the serious risks adjacent to the job conversion, of which the employment agencies do not inform them enough.

Second, they are innocent enough to realize the stringent economic fact that the surge of FDI deprives of the substantive parts of their jobs and lowers their wages. They misunderstand that the reason why they cannot be employed is in them. They are much eager to master some trifle 'skills' and get 'qualifications' which are likely become obsolete.

Thus, since the deep-rooted macroeconomic cause, which makes Japanese labor market for the youths so bearish, is concocted, every student and his or her parents are almost off track due to the factitious and frivolous advertisement of job mediation companies. Such an obscure and restless situation continues from the beginning of this century. Many Japanese become mutually insincere and are urged to the awful cutthroat competitions. As such, they evoke the appearance of strong despots whom they consider capable of leading them back to the stable growth economy.

1.4.2   *The prevalence of populism in economic policies*

This subsection analyzes the incautious inflation-recommending monetary policy in relation to the domestic fiscal crisis. Such a ceaseless expansionary monetary policy is advocated in conjunction with the political slogan 'Evacuation from the Deflation' (Defle Dakkyaku). As we shall precisely show in the Chapter 2, the progress of deflation is factitious and the price level (measured by CPI) is kept stable during the Structural Reformation Era and thereafter (see Figure 1.2). Then, why does such a frivolous advocacy prevail among most Japanese citizens?

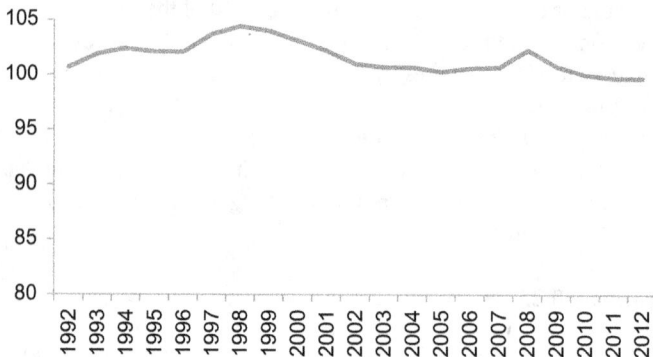

Figure 1.2 The time series of Japanese CPI

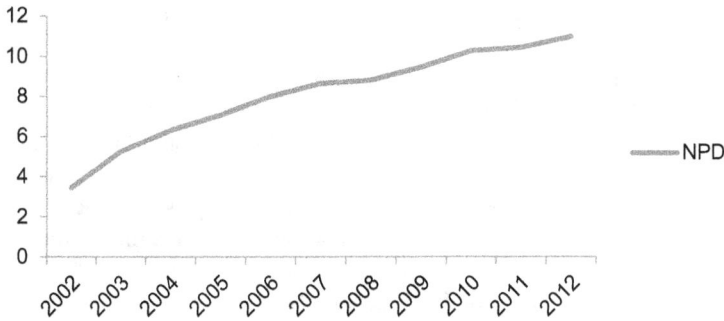

Figure 1.3 The accumulation of non-performing debt

To understand these politico-economic situations, we must note that the political slogan 'Evacuation from the Deflation' does not intend to evacuate from the deflation, which does not actually occur, but to boost the inflation. Thus, the question is why the government sticks to the inflationary policy, even disguising that Japanese economy falls into deflation.

There are two reasons that people believe that the inflation-recommending policy is effective as a measure for business upturn. People are erroneously persuaded that the inflation enriches their living standards because their diminishing nominal wages were salvaged by the inflation. As will be discussed in Chapter 2, there is no established theory which proves that the inflation enriches employees' income, because there is no guarantee that employers offer higher *real* wages even though they earn more *nominal* profits. The standard theory tells us the converse causality, that is, an upturn in business brings about the inflation. This is because the tightened labor markets push up nominal wages, and such increments of the production cost are reflected in the prices of goods.

The second reason is more serious one. The inflation substantively deducts the borrowers' burden. For example, as illustrated in Figure 1.3, the non-performing debts in the housing market soar from the Kozo Kaikaku Era.[6] Lessened wages and ceaseless downturns in land prices exacerbate this tendency. As such, boosting inflation reduces their debts in the real term.

However, whenever we realize that our properties are mostly or ultimately accumulated as the Japanese public debts, the interest incomes and face values which are fixed by the nominal term, the credibility and market values of our properties are heavily injured by the above-mentioned inflation-recommending policy based on populism. Such a policy is more harm than good as discussed in Chapter 2.

1.4.3   *The disillusion to the vagueness of the Japanese democracy*

The last factor, which induces the appalling despotic capitalism, is the revelation of the deceptiveness of so-called Post-War Democracy, which was mainly advocated by the left wing (the former Japanese Socialist Party and the Japanese

Communist Party). Although it is undeniable that the left wing played some sub-stantial political role to suppress the precarious chauvinism existing in the right wing of the Liberal Democrat Party, which revives both in the Koizumi and Abe cabinets, they had no alternative and structural view towards which the Japanese economy should advance.

Even after socialism revealed itself as a kind of despotism,[7] the parities would not change their negative views on the market economy and they are ever unable to accept the social democratic view that the government should help and tame the market economy to achieve the social cohesion, which is the central concept of Keynes' economics.[8]

Such inabilities became prominent during the Hatoyama and Kan cabinets of the Democratic Party from September 2009 to September 2011. They substan-tively and uncritically succeeded the deregulation policies railed by the Koizumi cabinet. Moreover, Prime Minister Yukio Hatoyama, who is not a socialist, upset the transition plan of the Futemma Base without any political preparation. This incautious behavior based on the populism, which is peculiar to the left wing not only made all residents of Okinawa thrown into the grievance, but also distilled the incredulous relationship to the United States.

Prime Minister Naoto Kan gave several provocative speeches on the historical relationship between Japan and the East Asian economies, and furies ensued both in Japan and overseas. These speeches brought about the same sort of unneces-sary political turbulences as Prime Minister Junichiro Koizumi and Shinzo Abe provoked from the opposite political side. In conjunction with unwise economic prospects and policies, such incessant and futile political disputes disillusioned the existence of the Democratic Party as the anti–right wing substance. More seriously, these make the legitimacy of democracy per se incredulous. Many Japanese, specifically those who have not been cultivated enough, come to seek a despot whom they believe is omnipotent and could solve every difficulty that Japan faces.

Such a deep incredulity towards the left wing and the democracy per se has been more seriously reflected in the dispute about the Japan Constitution. The cornerstone of the Japanese Democracy is the pacifistic Japan Constitution. Most of disputes concerning the intra–post war historical relationship to East Asian countries between the right wing and the minor left wing are rooted from the legitimacy of the Constitution, mainly from that of Article 9 of the Japanese Con-stitution, which swears that Japan abandons any war as a measure to dissolve any international conflict.

Article 9 of the Japanese Constitution is the most progressive thought of which Japanese should be proud. It is based on the devastating and tragic experiences from 1931 (the beginning of the Chino-Japan war without declaration) to 1945 (the end of the World War II). There is no doubt that any war is a vice in the fol-lowing two senses.

The first is, needless to say, its inhumanity. Since any thought should be sub-ject to humanism, it is not too much exaggerated to assert the preciousness of the peace. However, most Japanese are unable to have sufficient opportunities for the persuasive and commensurate discussion on this subject because it has been 70 years since Japan lost the war.

In conjunction with strenuous relationships to China and South Korea, chauvinism, which is concocted as an outlet for the discontent with the depressive economic environment, captivates many Japanese. As such, another measure for persuasion is indispensable to preserve Japanese Democracy, which is the acute miller image of the social coherent capitalism. This is closely connected with the second point on the vice of war.

The second point belongs to the economic sphere of the Article 9 of the Japanese Constitution, which is unfamiliar with many people but possesses the intrinsic economic value. There are two positive aspects in Article 9 from the fair economic percept. One is direct and calculable. The other is indirect and incalculable.

The direct one is the effect which economizes unnecessary heavy armament. In conjunction with this effect, we must note that the fiscal conditions of the Japanese government become serious. That is, huge amount of public debts (about 130 trillion yen at 2014) is accumulated via the persistent fiscal deficits (about 3 trillion yens measured by the primary balance).

If Article 9 of the Japanese Constitution is abolished, it will be certain that the military expenditure (Boei-Kankei-hi: about 4500 billion yens at 2013, which amounts to 5 per cent of the total fiscal expenditure) is substantively surcharged nominally on account of keeping the Japanese border from the menus of China. We need some precautions on such a half-cooked geopolitical discussion, which surely aggravates the economic relationship of Japan with the East Asian economies.

In addition, although slightly reduced year by year, the resume of the military expenditure in itself is quite precarious when we find ourselves facing the drastic aging and population-decreasing problem. The aging problem acclaim the more heavy tax burden on each citizen, even though the fiscal expenditure is kept intact. If the government myopically wants to evade such a difficulty, this ushers the bankruptcy of Japan by the cumulative and incessant accumulation of public debts, as shown in the previous section. As such, Article 9 of the Japan Constitution can be regard as a powerful bumper against the substantive inflammatory fiscal expansion caused by the military expansion and the serious aging problem.

The indirect economic well-being, which the Article 9 of the Japanese Constitution reveals, is to save Japan from unnecessary political strains with the East Asian economies and to progress the intimate economic relationship to them. Actually, no less East Asian people potentially hold the military menus from Japan, which stems from their tragic experiences during the World War II.

Whereas it is also certain that such hostility fades away in conjunction with the improvement in the economic relationship during the post-war to some extent, we should stringently recognize the acute fact that politicians in these countries always have the option to inflate such hostility to mitigate the domestic discontents on their own economy. We can find such prototype of the disputes in the recent strains with China and South Korea.

It is almost obvious that the revision or abolishment of the Article 9 of the Japanese Constitution will provoke the potential hostility of the East Asian economies to Japan, and thus, this provides the rightwing Abe cabinet with an excuse for enlarging the military expenditure. As mentioned above, such a strayed policy will surely endanger the sustainability of the Japanese economy.

In addition, whereas there are many serious conflicts, we must note that Japanese and East Asian economies are closely interdependent. Once the function of these stable relationships is paralyzed by the fanatic chauvinism, the stagnation to which the Japanese economy faces becomes more serious even though most Japanese firms decide to neither heavily depend on FDI nor seek their market into overseas. Thus the Article 9 of the Japanese Constitution is an overt cornerstone for preventing such unwise fiscal and foreign policies. This is the indirect and incalculable economic value of the ninth clause.

1.5   Concluding remarks

This section summarizes the discussion in this chapter.

1. Some social orders are required for a market economy to work as a social cohesion system, which means that people can enjoy maximal pleasure attainable subject to limited resources. One is the respect for the private property rights. Since the market mechanism owes to the individual motive to economize every limited resource to enjoy the life, the private property rights should be rigorously guaranteed. The other condition is to provide everyone with equal politico-economic opportunities. If someone is unable to access the market in which he or she wishes to participate, this person is obliged to plan his or her enjoyment subject to an unreasonably added constraint. Thus, if the equal opportunity is not guaranteed, the market economy fails to provide the maximal attainable pleasure.

2. The Structural Reformation (Kozo Kaikaku) advanced the destruction of the social orders under which the market economy operates soundly. We must note that some regulations are inevitable to keep the orders required for sustaining the market economy. Most deregulation policies, which characterize the Structural Reformation discussed above, are the very destructions of such orders. We call such disordered market economy the despotic capitalism.

3. The capital market is genetically imperfect in the sense that a lender is unable to know the borrower's revenue from various investments (including educational investments) completely. Hence, the evidence of the depth of the commitment to the investment is vital for accessing the capital market. The amount of one's own funds is regarded as a decisive signal because it represents the borrower's loss when the default occurs. Accordingly, banks never lend money to those who do not possess affluent funds.

4. Presuming such an imperfection in the capital market, the labor market is deregulated. Many youths are forced to fight with the lower-wage countries. Even though a high-teenage worker wishes to enter a university and improve his or her abilities, if his or her lowered wage cannot lead to sufficient savings, such person is unable to finance the tuition lending from a bank. Thus,

the deregulation of the labor market is acutely disadvantageous especially for the youths. Such a severe reality amplifies the tendency among youths that only the wealthy strata are respectful although they are the despots that annoy them.

5. The effect of industrial hollowing owing to the surge of FDI to the labor market is extremely underestimated. In conjunction with the obscure and ephemeral information on the labor market, almost every youth misunderstands his or her situation within the labor market. This surely heightens the unemployment of the youths.

6. The inability of the Democratic Party reveals the deceptiveness of the postwar left wing. This annihilates the belief in the importance of democracy, and many Japanese eagerly desire the arrival of despots, who are omnipotent to any difficulty. As such, the despotic capitalism further advances adjacent to the fanatic chauvinism.

Notes

1 One must note that there is an overt inconsistency within the BOJ's assertions concerning the monetary policy during the era of Bubble Economy and during the factitious 'deflation era,' which will be dealt in the next section. It is apparent that the CPI was stable throughout both eras. However, the BOJ preferred the accommodative laissez-faire policy during the Bubble Economy. On the other hand, the BOJ is eager for the active interventions against the will in money markets for accelerating the inflation despite the fact that the Law of Bank of Japan prescribes its main mandatory as the stabilization of prices.

2 The data sources are the statements of profit and loss, and the balance sheets of the New Bank Tokyo.

3 RAD is the ratio of capital expenditure abroad to domestic capital expenditure within manufacture industry. The data sources are 'Survey on Planned Capital Expenditure for Fiscal Year' provided by the Development Bank of Japan.

4 The reason why most part of profits earned by FDI is unrealizable and spurious is analyzed in detail in Chapters 5 and 6.

5 More precise discussion on this subject, for example, see Stiglitz and Weiss (1981). Otaki (2014) argues the effects of the incompleteness of the capital market to educational investment.

6 Data Source: Disclosure Journal of Japan Housing Finance Agency. NPD is the ratio of non-performing debts to the total loan.

7 See Arendt (1968) and Carr (1979) for more detail on the governance theory of socialism as despotism.

8 Keynes' excellent thought is characterized by not only logical consistency and permeated liberal viewpoint but also its relevance which gets along with the concurrent politico-economic situation where Britain once was. His thought is far wider and deeper than that in Keynes (1936). See, for example, Keynes (2013).

References

Arendt, H. (1968) *The Origins of Totalitarianism* [New Edition with Added Prefaces]. San Diego: A Harvest Book Harcourt Brace & Company. [originally published in 1948]

Carr, E. H. (1979) *The Russian Revolution from Lenin to Stalin (1917–1929)*. London: Macmillan.

Keynes, J. M. (1936) *The General Theory of Employment, Interest and Money.* London: Macmillan.

Keynes, J. M. (2013) *Activities 1931–1939: World Crises and Policies in Britain and America.* In *The Collected Writings of John Maynard Keynes XXI,* Edited by D. Moggridge. Cambridge, UK: Cambridge University Press.

Okina, K. (1993) *Kinyu Seisaku: Chuo-Ginko no Shiten to Sentaku* (The Monetary Policy: The Viewpoint and the Choice of the Central Bank). Tokyo, Japan: Toyo Keizai Shipo-sha.

Otaki, M. (2014) Efficacy in education and intergenerational wellbeing. *Theoretical Economics Letters, 4,* 183–189.

Stiglitz, J. E. and A. Weiss (1981). Credit rationing in markets with imperfect information. *American Economic Review, 81,* 393–410.

Part II

The macroeconomic policies in the prolonged economic stagnation

This part deals with current monetary policy in Japan. Particularly, we explore why the policy makers stick to inflationary policy. One will find that such a policy not only fails to overcome the prominent disinflation, but is also precarious. Our final goal is to analyze where the ineffectiveness and precariousness of ongoing monetary policy come from.

2 Devastating consequences of the busted Bubble and frivolous advocacy of deflation

2.1 Devastating consequences of the busted Bubble

2.1.1 The definition of the fundamental values of a typical residence

Generally, a bubble asset price is defined as the discrepancy between its current market price and its fundamental value. While the market value is observable, the fundamental value is not. Hence we must estimate the value relying on some plausible assumptions.

We here presume the capital-market imperfection for estimating the fundamental value of a typical residence in the following sense. Every individual cannot borrow money beyond his or her discount sum of lifetime savings. For an elementary and naïve economics, such a borrowing constraint suggests the existence of capital-market imperfectness. If we can regard an individual's family as a kind of dynasty, he or she can borrow infinite sum of money in exchange for his or her descendants' incomes. The reason why an individual is unable to borrow such huge amounts of money and loses the advantageous investment opportunities owes much to the imperfectness of information about his or her descendants' abilities and incomes.

Although such kind of assertion is far beyond reality and apparently trespasses descendants' property rights, lay economists proclaim that this is a capital-market imperfection, which must be cured and actually can be overcome. Accordingly, whenever they calculate the fundamental value of an asset, they entirely rely on the fictitious capital-market's completeness.

In contrast with this definition, we instead assume that the capital market is genetically incomplete, and the financial intermediaries are unable to lend money beyond one's life. Furthermore, the scrap value of a residence (i.e., the value of the residence when the long-term loan is completely redeemed) is assumed to be negligible. This assumption is natural when we take account of the huge costs of renovation for the residence that is unavoidable. Based on these two assumptions, we shall calculate the fundamental values of a typical residence of the Bubble Era (1994) and Post-Bubble Era (2012), although they are round numbers.

2.1.2   The estimated divergence of the market value of a typical residence from its fundamental value

In the following estimations, mainly simplifying the analysis, we assume that once an individual purchases the typical residence, he or she only can resell it at the fundamental price. This assumption is not far from reality at first glance. Because our fundamental value of the typical residence is defined as the utmost price at which another rational individual (we call him a rationalist), can purchase the residence. Accordingly, a seller, who once feverishly dreamed about the explosion of the residence price, only can find the offer of the rationalist. As such, our simplifying assumption is almost justified.

The estimation method of the fundamental value of a typical residence at 1994 and 2012 is as follows.

Assumptions

1. Based on the Survey of Household Economy (Statistics Bureau, Ministry of Internal Affairs and Communications), we estimate the annual residential loan repayment per employee's family from 2004 to 2012. These figures are rather stable and range from 1.40 to 1.77 million JPYs. The averaged payment within recent four years is about 1.70 million JPYs. We regard this value as the actual sum of the loan repayment of 2012.
2. Since the data concerning the loan repayment of 1994 are unavailable, we estimate the value by the following procedure: first, we calculate the repayment/disposable-income ratio relying on the data from 2004 to 2012. These values are quite stable. It is located within 0.28–0.34, and thus we assign this value 0.3. The disposable income during 1994 is knowable and amounts to 3.9 million JPYs. Consequently, we infer the sum of the repayment per annum during 1994, $3.9 \times 0.3 \approx 1.2$ (million JPYs)
3. The loan interest rates offered by Japan Housing Finance Agency (Jutaku Shien Kio) are publicized. Each rate during 1994 and 2012 is 5.0 and 2.5 per cent, respectively.
4. The averaged squares of a residence are kept astonishingly stable. The values are 64.6m^2 in 1994 and 64.3m^2 in 2012, respectively (the datum of 1994 is based on Fukuda (2010). The value at 2012 is estimated from the Survey of Household Economy). Hence we fixed the occupied areas at 64.5 m^2 throughout time.
5. The market values of the typical residence per square meter are 0.68 million JPYs (1994 by Fukuda (2010)) and 0.65 million JPYs (2012 by the Research Institute of Immobile Assets: Fudosan Keizai Kenkyujo), and thus we fixed the market value at 0.67 million JPY.
6. We assume that the typical loan is entirely redeemed in 30 years.

The result of the estimation

Based on the above assumptions, we can calculate the hypothetical fundamental value F subject to the following formula:

$$F = L \times \frac{1 - \left[\dfrac{1}{1+r}\right]^{30}}{1 - \dfrac{1}{1+r}} \tag{2.1}$$

where L is the fundable loan which is estimated by the methods in Assumption 1 and 2, and hence

$$L = 1.2(1994), \ 1.7(2012) \tag{2.2}$$

r is the interest rate accrued by the loan. Thus, from the evidence in Assumption 3, we get

$$r = 0.05(1994), \ 0.025(2012) \tag{2.3}$$

Substituting (2.2) and (2.3) into (2.1), we obtain the following estimation of the fundamental value of the typical residence. That is,

$$F \approx 19 \, (million \, JPY)(1994), \ 36 \, (million \, JPY)(2012) \tag{2.4}$$

Next, we calculate the market value of the typical new residence using Assumptions 4 and 5. Astonishingly, perhaps owing to oligopolistic price strategies (e.g., an implicit price-maintaining curtail) of the housing industry, there is no substantive change in the market price during these 20 years. The market value M is

$$M = 0.67 \times 64.5 \approx 43 \, (millionJPYs) \tag{2.5}$$

Subtracting (2.4) from (2.5), we obtain how far the market value diverges from the fundamental value. That is,

$$M - F = 24 \, (millionJPY : 1994), \ 7 \, (millionJPY : 2012) \tag{2.6}$$

These figures imply that our typical residence was overvalued by 125 per cent during 1994, and by 19 per cent even during 2012. Moreover, this evidence suggests that those who purchase typical residences are heavily indebted. Since their averaged disposable income is 3.9 million JPYs during 1994 (Assumption 2), they hold unredeemable money by 6.15(that is, 24/3.9) times of their annual disposable income. This amount is apparently far beyond their solvency. Such estimation is coincident with Figure 1.3 in Chapter 1, which illustrates the heap of the non-performing debts held by Japan Housing Finance Agency.

As illustrated above, although this is only a small portion of the non-performing debts, we can sufficiently infer how seriously the busted Bubble still negatively affects the Japanese economy even 20 years later. Since inflation lightens the burden of heavy indebtedness, potential desires for injustice and feverish inflationary monetary policy are advocated mainly by the Japanese mass media.

Caveats

We need some caveats on the estimation of the fundamental values.

1. Although the fundable loan increases from 1.2 million JPYs (1994) to 1.7 million JPY (2012), it is possibly overestimated, and so is the fundamental value in 2012. This is because there are possibilities that indebted individuals might be forced to increase their loan payments to compensate their disappointed capital losses. That is, the abnormal discrepancy between the market and fundamental values during the Bubble Era cannot be explained without feverish and rootless expectations on the capital gains from immobile assets.
2. The market value in 2012 might be rather overestimated in reality. According to the Land Price Index provided by Sanyu System Appraisal (2013), the land price decreased 40 per cent from 1994 to 2012. It is natural that the price of our typical residence (i.e., the residence price when the loan is entirely repaid) is affected by such downturn.
3. The scrap value of the residence is neglected by assumption. Caveat 2, which indicates that there is substantial fall in the land price during these 20 years, the upturn of the fundamental price might be not as large as the estimator reveals.

However, even if we admit that such precautions are necessary, it is undeniable that the unforeseeable overestimation of immobile assets is still heavily injuring the Japanese economy, and thus this closely connects with the advocacy of the inflationary monetary policy.

2.2   The prominence of disinflation throughout the post-war Japanese economy

This section considers the long-run price level movement of the post-war Japanese economy. We will find that the advance of deflation in current Japanese economy is fictitious. This fact also helps to reveal the reason why the inflation-promoting monetary policy is incessantly scattered by the mass media in conjunction with the huge amounts of non-performing debts that is analyzed in the previous section in more detail.

At the beginning, it is necessary to make a distinction between *disinflation* and *deflation.*

Definitions

1. *Disinflation is a price-level movement in which the inflation rate continuously falls. Deflation is possibly caused as the consequence of disinflation.*
2. *Deflation is a price-level movement in which the inflation rate takes some significantly negative value.*

Thus, disinflation does not always imply deflation and vice versa. This distinction will be crucial for the analysis below.

Table 2.1 Ten-year averaged inflation rate (%) and unemployment rate (%)

	1960s	*1970s*	*1980s*	*1990s*	*2000s*
Inflation rate	5.6	4.1	1.8	1.0	−0.3
Unemployment rate	1.3	1.7	2.5	3.1	4.6

Data source: Statistic Bureau, Ministry of Internal Affairs and Communications

Table 2.2 The Consumer Price Index (CPI) during the Showa Depression

	1929s	*1930s*	*1931s*	*1932*	*1933*	*1934*	*1935*
CPI	100	89.8	79.5	80.4	82.9	84.0	86.1

Data source: Long Term Economic Statistics provided by the Institute of Economic Research, Hitotsubashi University

2.2.1 *Some historical evidence*

Table 2.1 shows the 10-year averaged inflation rate measured by the Consumer Price Index (CPI) and the averaged unemployment rate during the post-war era. We can easily find that the disinflation is quite prominent throughout these five decades. The inflation rate decreases by approximately 1 per cent point during each decade. Japanese economy slightly tilts towards deflation after the new century (−0.3 per cent). However, it rather stays within the statistical measurement error, and thus we should regard the price level (CPI) as stable after the 1980s.

This assertion becomes quite clear when we refer the harsh deflation during the Showa Depression, which originated from the Great Depression in the United States. Table 2.2 indicates how severe the deflation was. During the first two years of the Depression, the inflation rate was around −10 per cent and never recovered within the available sample periods.

As such, we can easily imagine that the current faint deflation is quite different in its nature and causation from that in the Showa Depression that occurred some 80 years ago. We shall deal with these problems precisely in Chapter 3. At any rate, we must note that it is indispensable to distinguish the cruelty of the deflation during the Showa Depression from the almost harmless deflation during our prolonged stagnation era rigorously. In addition, from the long-run viewpoint, what characterizes the post-war Japanese economy is not the shortsighted deflation, but the long-run disinflation throughout this era.

2.2.2 *A hidden political will embodied in the advocate of 'evacuation from the deflation' (Defure Dakkyaku)*

Against the fact that there was no serious deflation during the post-Bubble Era, almost all politicians agree on 'Evacuation from the Deflation' regardless of their affiliation. Such a shameful phenomenon partly reflects their idleness and/or ignorance when it comes to current Japanese economy.

However, we must note that many politicians in current Japan are de facto advocates for the intension of the wealthy stratum, and rotten to a kind of marionettes of the mass media. As estimated above, most individuals who were in speculative position during the Bubble Era are heavily indebted, independent whether or not they are affluent. The lands and the stocks are quite lucrative assets, and thus the investment opportunities to such assets are far more abundant for the wealthy stratum than for non-wealthy strata.

It implies that those who are in more dismay positions in current Japan are considered to be wealthy individuals, who have vital influence to the Japanese mass media and politicians subdued by them. It is natural to judge the relevance of the popular political slogan 'Evacuation from the Deflation' from such a context. That is, the propaganda 'Evacuation from the Deflation' is fictitious, and it really aims to trigger and progress inflation.

This is because inflation lightens the burdens of nominally fixed debts. Nevertheless, we must realize that inflation is a kind of tax. Although those who bothered by heavy indebtedness owing to the failure of the speculation are emancipated from their burden, it is quite harmful for most of sound individuals whose properties comprise the nominal assets such as bank deposits, postal savings (the postal saving is a peculiar system in Japan that post offices provide deposit), and public debts, etc.

In other words, the progress of inflation amplifies the inequality of wealth via the hidden income transfer from the lower income individuals to wealthy ones. Thus, the propaganda 'Evacuation from the deflation' is quite precarious whenever we remind ourselves of the fact that the inflation tax is extremely digressive.

To summarize, the widely prevalent slogan 'Evacuation from the Deflation' is not only against the statistical evidences, but also quite appalling for most innocuous citizens because it hides the intention to promote inflation that is an acutely digressive tax on its back.

2.3   Is inflation really a monetary phenomenon? There is no consistent theory which advocates that inflation upturns the business

2.3.1   Captives of the quantity theory of money

Most economists are captives of the quantity theory of money. They tend to think that prices of goods proportionately and uniformly increase with the quantity of money, although there might be some lags for realigning the prices in reality.

The most prominent feature of this thesis is the *disbelief in the intrinsic value of money*. The advocates of the quantity theory (including 'new Keynesians') regard money as only a measure for values of various goods. Accordingly, as far as new issues are proportionately distributed in accordance with their existing money stocks, the prices are determined in proportion to the aggregate monetary stock because such an increase in money supply is equivalent to some kind of denomination. This is the vital reason why current light-headed economists eagerly recommend the expansionary monetary policy to promote inflation via various channels.

Definition

We call that money is in disbelief when the value of money proportionately decreases with the quantity.[1]

However, we must note that if money is only the measure of value, it is unable to circulate. This is because, unless money is storable, it becomes worthless soon after the current transactions are completed. Since every individual is correctly afraid that he becomes the last owner of money, and there is equal probability to encounter such a hard case, nobody wants to receive money beforehand. Thus, money never circulates without the role of stores of value.

Let us, instead, assume that money is storable and that individuals have some *confidence* in the future value of money. Then, there it is not inevitable that prices proportionately vary with the current nominal money supply. That is, individuals *believe* the intrinsic value of money which might be independent of the quantity of money.

Although this seems a curious assumption at a glance, it is closely intimate to our daily experiences. We usually deposit substantive money to bank and use credit cards on the basis of such confidence. It implies that we are *confident* of the future intrinsic value of money in terms of goods because we believe that value does not depreciate so easily. In addition, we scarcely take notice of a change in the aggregate money supply when we decide our economic activities. If the quantity theory of money were upheld, such information would be crucial for anticipating the inflation. This evidence suggests that it is thinkable that individuals normally *believe* the intrinsic value of money which is independent of the aggregate money supply.

Next, we turn to what happens when individuals are confident in the future value of money and the quantity theory is not upheld. For simplicity, we assume that goods also serve as stores of value without depletion. Then, the rate of return for a unit of goods is

$$\frac{1}{1} = 1 \tag{2.7}$$

When individuals are confident in the future intrinsic value of money independent of the aggregate money supply, the value is

$$\frac{1}{p_{t+1}}$$

where p_{t+1} is the future price level.[2] Hence the rate of return for money is

$$\frac{\frac{1}{p_{t+1}}}{\frac{1}{p_t}} = \frac{p_t}{p_{t+1}} \tag{2.8}$$

It is the necessary and sufficient condition for both money and goods that the rates of return are equalized. Thus, from (2.7) and (2.8), we obtain

$$\frac{p_t}{p_{t+1}} = 1 \Leftrightarrow p_t = \overline{p_{t+1}} \tag{2.9}$$

Equation 2.9 implies that whenever individuals trust the future intrinsic value of money $\frac{1}{p_{t+1}}$, current price p_t also is kept constant at the level of $\overline{p_{t+1}}$ and becomes independent of the quantity of money.

Thus, we obtain the following definition.

Definition

> *We say individuals are confident of (or believe) the intrinsic value of money when their rational expectations on the future price level are unrelated to the quantity of money.*

Closing this subsection, let us examine how the disbelief and the confidence affect the real economy. The key concept for this analysis is the real cash balance $\frac{M_t}{p_t}$, where M_t is the quantity of money. The real cash balance represents the aggregate purchasing power of money. In other words, the real cash balance corresponds to how many goods are obtainable in exchange for the existing money stock.

Let us use a simple numerical example to exhibit the contrast between the case for *disbelief* in the value of money and that for the *confidence*. Assume, in both states, that the economy is initially located at

$$M_t = 1, p_t = 1 \Rightarrow \frac{M_t}{p_t} = 1 \tag{2.10}$$

Next, consider that the quantity of money is doubled, then,

$$M_t = 2, p_t = 2 \Rightarrow \frac{M_t}{p_t} = 1 \tag{2.11}$$

holds when the *disbelief* is prevalent and the quantity theory holds. On the other hand, if individuals are confident

$$M_t = 2, p_t = 1 \Rightarrow \frac{M_t}{p_t} = 2 \tag{2.12}$$

Thus, only when individuals are confident of the intrinsic value of money, the business in the economy upturns by some modest monetary expansion (the above example is too exaggerated for simplifying the calculation) because they become able to purchase more goods as far as there are idling resources in the economy.

Accordingly, maintaining the confidence of the intrinsic value of money is crucial for keeping the monetary policy effective. Such policy as urging the inflation expectations, which the BOJ currently is eagerly progressing, is quite dangerous in the sense that it possibly harms the *confidence* of money.

2.3.2 The nest theory of the value of money: a heuristic derivation of the fundamental equation of the monetary economy

In the previous subsection, we have shown the unreality of the quantity theory of money. Then, how are the price level and the inflation rate determined? This subsection deals with this problem.

In the standard microeconomic theory, as Keynes (1936) emphasizes, prices are governed by their production costs, which mainly comprise the wage costs. It is very curious that the quantity of money suddenly appears as the decisive factor for the price level determination. Thus, there is a serious rift between the micro-economic and macroeconomic theories.[3]

We shall reconstruct a price theory in the monetary economy which is consistent with the firm's economic behavior in conjunction with the concept of the confidence of money introduced in the previous subsection.

Then, let us denote the price level p_t and the labor productivity γ during period t, respectively. The current nominal wage paid for an individual W_t depends on both p_t and p_{t+1} if individuals live during two periods: present and future. Thus, we can write

$$W_t = W\left(p_t, p_{t+1}\right) \tag{2.13}$$

We must note that when prices uniformly rise, for example rise twice, the required wage for keeping individuals work also doubles. That is,

$$W\left(2p_t, 2p_{t+1}\right) = 2W\left(p_t, p_{t+1}\right) \tag{2.14}$$

Since goods are produced by the amount of y per capita, the unit cost of the production of the goods is

$$W_t \div \gamma = \frac{W\left(p_t, p_{t+1}\right)}{\gamma} \tag{2.15}$$

We can easily show that oligopolistic firms determine their output prices by add-ing up some margin θ on the unit production cost.[4] Hence, by using Equation 2.15, we finally obtain

$$p_t = \left[1 + \theta\right]\frac{W\left(p_t, p_{t+1}\right)}{\gamma} \tag{2.16}$$

This is *the fundamental equation of the monetary economy*. This equation has two following prominent characteristics.

1. **The nested structure:** the rational expectation on the future price level p_{t+1} determines the current price level p_t. That is, the value of money is deter-mined by how individuals evaluate its future value.

2.   **The irrelevance of the quantity of money:** since the current quantity of money M_t does not appear in the fundamental Equation 2.16, it never affects the price levels. In other words, if money is confident and p_{t+1} fixed by some value $\bar{p}$, the current price level is determined so as to satisfy the fundamental Equation 2.16 independently of M_t.

Thus, the numerical example in 2.3.1 can be justified by the employees and employers rational economic behaviors and expectations summarized in the fundamental Equation 2.16.

2.3.3   *Inflation is a real phenomenon when an economy falls into the imperfect employment*

We shall try to analyze the fundamental Equation 2.16 in more detail. Let us remind of the nominal wage which is enough to incentivize employees. $W\left(p_t, p_{t+1}\right)$ has the property in Equation 2.14. This time, we replace the value 2 with $\frac{1}{p_t}$. Then, we obtain

$$W\left(\frac{p_t}{p_t}, \frac{p_{t+1}}{p_t}\right) = \frac{1}{p_t} W\left(p_t, p_{t+1}\right) \Leftrightarrow W\left(1, \frac{p_{t+1}}{p_t}\right) = \frac{1}{p_t} W\left(p_t, p_{t+1}\right)$$

$$\Leftrightarrow W\left(p_t, p_{t+1}\right) = p_t \cdot W\left(1, \frac{p_{t+1}}{p_t}\right) \tag{2.17}$$

Substituting Equation 2.17 into the fundamental Equation 2.16, we can find the following relationship between the inflation rate $\frac{p_{t+1}}{p_t}$ and the labor productivity γ:

$$p_t = \frac{[1+\theta] p_t \cdot W\left(1, \frac{p_{t+1}}{p_t}\right)}{\gamma} \Leftrightarrow \gamma = [1+\theta] \cdot W\left(1, \frac{p_{t+1}}{p_t}\right) \tag{2.18}$$

The nominal wage W increases with the advance of inflation because employees should be compensated from the depletion of the value of money. Hence the right-hand side of Equation 2.18 increases with the inflation rate $\frac{p_{t+1}}{p_t}$. As a result, whenever the labor productivity γ progresses, the inflation accelerates. Accordingly, inflation is not the monetary phenomenon as the quantity theory asserts, but the real one when the economy hoards idling resources as discussed in Section 2.3.1.

2.3.4   *The slowdown of the labor productivity progress causes the disinflation*

In the previous subsection, we have shown the positive causality from the labor productivity to the inflation rate (the positive causality means that the progress of the labor productivity enhances the inflation). However, this is derived rather mechanically and mathematically. In this subsection, we provide the economic meaning of such causality.

There are two important economic facts in relation to this causality.

1. For any rationally expected future price level p_{t+1}, the current price level p_t is relatively lowered because of the progress of the labor productivity γ. This is the cost reduction effect of the increase in γ. This fact conversely implies that the inflation is accelerated in conjunction with the labor productivity progress except for the change in the current price level p_t.
2. Assume that the initial progress of the labor productivity is entirely absorbed by the proportionate increase in the nominal wage W_t. Then the current price level p_t is kept unchanged (see Equation 2.16). This fact implies that the current value of money, which is defined by $\frac{1}{p_t}$, is kept unchanged whenever the nominal wage perfectly reflects the progress of the labor productivity.

Combining these two facts, we attain the following proposition.

Proposition

> *If the nominal wage proportionately increases with the progress of the labor supply, such progress associates the sequential depletion of values of money.*

Thus, the cost reduction effect, which comes from a progress in the labor productivity, is absorbed by the dearer wages, and results in depleting values of money.[5]

In turn, it is thinkable that the disinflation, which characterizes the post-war Japanese economy and most prominent during these 20 years as precisely depicted in Section 2.2, is caused by the descending of the labor productivity progress (see Table 2.3).

That is, the slowdown of the labor productivity immediately induces the proportionate nominal wage cutting. The current price level is kept unchanged in such a case. Since the stagnation of the labor productivity also raises the current production cost, employees are impoverished since such a movement decreases the real wage. Accordingly, employers lower the price of goods from the next period and

Table 2.3 The stagnant labor productivity

	1980s	*1990s*	*2000s*
The Progress of the Labor Productivity (%)	0.70	−0.06	−0.3

Data source: Labor Productivity Index, Japan Productivity Center

(The actual labor productivity progressed by 1.06 per cent on average from 1980 to 2009. We regard this trend as the contribution of physical capital. By subtracting this trend from the actual value, we define the true labor productivity progress.)

thereafter than expected. Thus disinflation is brought about by the slowdown of the labor productivity.

From this point of view, the prominent disinflation in Japanese economy is not a monetary phenomenon caused by the shortage of the quantity of money, but a real phenomenon which comes from the stagnation of the labor productivity progress. In this sense, as already mentioned in Sections 2.2.2 and 2.3.1, the concurrent monetary policy by the BOJ, which unreasonably aims to promote inflation via perturbing the confidence of money, is quite precarious. Keynes (2013, p.104) asserts that '[a] policy of price stability is the very opposite of a policy of permanently cheap money.' One of his reasons (p. 117) is that '[m]odern individualistic society, organized on lines of capitalistic industry, cannot support a violently fluctuating standard of value, whether the movement is upwards or downwards. Its arrangements presume and absolutely require a reasonably stable standard.'

2.4   The stable long-run Phillips curve during the post-war Japanese economy

We have established the theory why the inflation rate positively correlates to the progress of the labor productivity. There comes the natural question what economic factor determines labor productivity. Although there are other economic factors (e.g., capital accumulation, product innovation and etc.), we assume that the labor productivity is acutely affected by the unemployment rate.

Figure 2.1 is the long-run Phillips curve of the Japanese economy reflecting the data in Table 2.1. We can clearly find that the Phillips curve is stable and downward-sloping. We must find the economic incidence which governs the progress of the labor productivity keeping consistency with the developed theory in Section 2.3.4 and this stable long-run Phillips curve.[6]

The hypothesis that the higher unemployment rate lowers the labor productivity satisfies such requirements: an upturn of the unemployment rate lowers the labor productivity, and from the Proposition in 2.3.4, the lowered labor productivity advances disinflation. Thus, there emerges the negative causality from the unemployment rate to the inflation rate.

We must show the reason why an increase in the unemployment rate lowers the labor productivity. As discussed in detail in Chapters 5 and 6, this might well relate to the accumulation process of the human capital. As Coase (1937) asserts, firm is an economic organization to dissolve problems which market is unable to do so. One of the most serious problems which firm has to dissolve is to promote the cooperation within the firm.

If jobs are decomposable (or standardized) in the sense that the firm can achieve the best outcome only by assigning each employee what he or she should do in his or her job description without communicating other employees, then the quality of labor forces within and without the firm is not distinguishable. As such, there is no necessity to organize the firm. It suffices for any would-be employer to collect the labor force in the *markets* as many as he hopes.

Inflation Rate

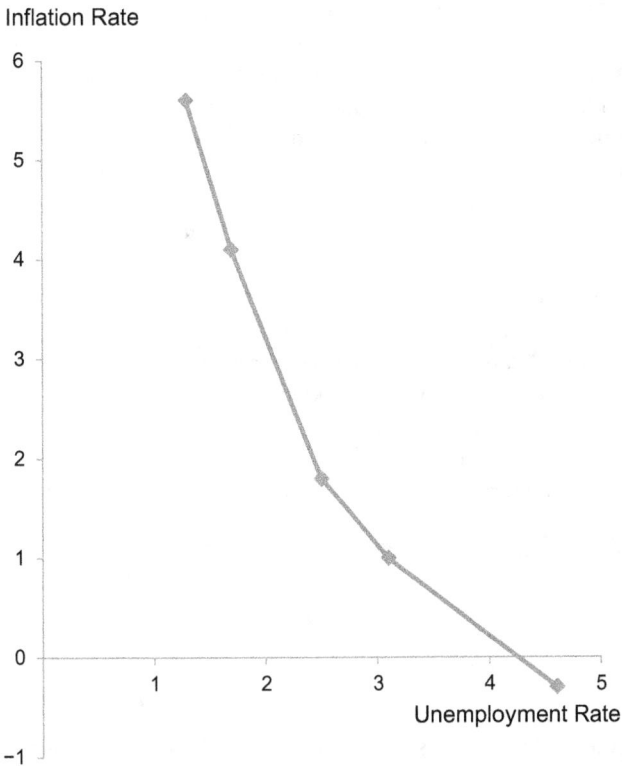

Figure 2.1 The long-run Phillips curve

However, boundaries of jobs are quite vague in reality, and each job is closely connected, and hence some mutual compensations and coordination within the firm are in acute necessity for managing the firm efficiently. Hence, abilities for the cohesion within an organization progresses the labor productivity as an entity.

These socialized abilities, which employees should have had when they enter the labor markets, are mainly nourished by the formal and informal education in elementary and secondary schools. In Japan, before the Structural Reformation (Kozo Kaikaku), even education in high schools, colleges and universities stress the importance on such abilities, although it may not take explicit forms.

Thus, how to enhance these abilities is the social problem which cannot be solved by a family and/or a firm. In this sense, the macroeconomic labor productivity is an exogenous variable for each economic agent, but is an endogenous variable within an economy as a whole.

As discussed in Section 1.2.3 and 2.1.1, the capital market is genetically imperfect mainly because an individual should never be collateralized from the view of the human right. However, this engulfs the disparity of income. Once a middle-aged householder loses his job (note that the unemployment time is quite long in

Japan), it becomes difficult for his children to access the higher educational opportunities. Moreover, the large reduction in income due to unemployment leads his family to an unstable daily life in many cases. This is quite harmful for his children to nourish their social characters. Thus, the macroeconomic labor productivity decreases with the unemployment rate in the long run.

It is also notable that the extension of the income disparity also affects the negative external effect even to the affluent class, which is not annoyed by the capital market imperfection. This is because the socialized characters necessary for efficient operations within the firm require the homogeneity of its constituents to some extent. When a kind of strata is affected by such an expansion, it makes the dense communication difficult across the strata and reduces the efficiency within the firm. This also lowers the labor productivity of the firm as an entity. Consequently, the rift caused by the disparity of income owing to the increase in the unemployment rate aggravates the productivity of labor.

To summarize, see the following flow chart.

The unemployment rate $\Uparrow$ $\Rightarrow$ The labor productivity $\Downarrow$ $\Rightarrow$ The inflation rate $\Downarrow$

Thus, we have dissolved why the stable downward long-run Phillips curve exists in Japan.

2.5   The vicious cycle

Concluding this chapter, we shall show why the stagnation is so prolonged in Japanese economy. The initial shock was the busted speculative bubble around 1991. Ensued fiscal expansions lead to the huge deficits rather than eased such an oppressive shock (see Table 1.2). As Table 2.4 indicates, Japan enjoyed the highly ranked gross domestic product per capita during the 1990s, although the unemployment rate rose 1 per cent.

These facts suggest that Japan was still enjoying the spurious prosperity in the 1990s against the political propaganda of 'The Lost Decade'. However, as its dark side, the fiscal soundness was undermined and the income disparity seriously progressed.

Entering into this century, and concurrently with the Structural Reformation (Kozo Kaikaku), the following vicious cycle becomes apparent. Further stimulus by the expansionary fiscal policy is hindered by the enormous accumulation of

Table 2.4 The average ranking of the GDP per capita within OECD countries

	1980s	1990s	2000s
The Ranking	9.80/26	4.4/34	12.4/34

Data source: OECD National Accounts Database (Note that the number of affiliates in OECD increases from 26 to 28 at 1990. It also increases 29 and 31 at 1991 and 1994, respectively. The present number 34 is from 1995.)

the public debt. In conjunction with the politically intended rapid progress of the foreign direct investment (FDI), effective demand in the domestic markets is remarkably thwarted.

This, in turn, aggravated the employment environment and further raised the unemployment rate. As discussed in Section 2.5, it caused the appalling stagnation of the labor productivity and adjoined the disinflation.

Disinflation generally curtails the consumption because individuals expect that they can purchase cheaper goods in the future. In conjunction with the decrease in the labor income, this accelerates the downturn of business. Then, the unemployment increases further, and thus the vicious cycle is closed.

The vicious cycle

The Busted Bubble and the Surge of FDI ⇒Stagnant Domestic Markets ⇒Unemployment ⇑⇒Labor Productivity ⇓ ⇒Disinflation ⇒Consumption ⇓ ⇒Stagnant Domestic Markets ⇒

We consider that the current Japanese economy is entrapped by this vicious cycle.

2.6 Concluding Remarks

We discuss how the speculative bubble from the late 1980s to the beginning of the 1990s affects Japanese economy afterward. The obtained results are as follows:

1. The price of the typical residence, in which a standard Japanese family lives, was overvalued about 2.2 times from the estimated fundamental value. Since the unrepayable debts brought about the bust of the bubble amount to about 5 times of the average disposable income per annum, it is unreal to regard the non-performing debt problem as having been settled, even more than 20 years have past after the bust. This still suppresses the consumption of individuals to non-negligible extent.
2. There is a prominent tendency of disinflation throughout the post-war Japanese economy. Although Japan experiences the slightly negative inflation rates around the turn of the century, it is improper to compare such negative inflation rates to the fierce deflation during the Showa Depression in the 1930s.
3. The long-run disinflation, which has been more prominent since the 1980s, comes from the stagnant labor productivity. There are two economic consequences of the labor productivity slowdown. First, it makes the unit production cost more expensive relatively to any arbitrarily given future cost. This is the dynamic cost–push effect of the labor productivity slowdown. Second, as far as the nominal wage is cut in accordance with the lowered productivity, the current price level is kept unchanged. Thus, the stagnation in the labor productivity brings about the lower real wage and the prevalence of disinflationary rational expectations.

4. The stagnation in labor productivity possibly comes from the upward tendency of the unemployment rate in the long run. The most notable tragic affair, which adjoins the unemployment, is the unstable family life due to the lowered income. Children, who grow under such a misfortune, in conjunction with the genetic capital market imperfection, would find much difficulty in nourishing their social characteristics. Since the mutual compensation and/or coordination within a firm depend on these characteristics, mass unemployment stagnate the labor productivity at least in the long run. Thus, we can explain the reason why the long-run Phillips curve of the Japanese economy is so stable.

5. The current Japanese economy is entrapped in the following vicious cycle:

    1. The huge capital loss by the bust of the bubble and the surge of FDI, as precisely analyzed in Chapter 6, lessens the domestic effective demand.
    2. Thwarted domestic demand increases the unemployment rate.
    3. The upturn in the unemployment rate erodes the labor productivity.
    4. The stagnation in the labor productivity distills the disinflationary expectations.
    5. The disinflation, in conjunction with the labor income reduction, advances the shrink of the domestic economy. The economy is entrapped the vicious cycle from (2) to (5).

Notes

1 The value of money is defined as the inverse of the price level. See below for discussion.
2 The value of money is defined by the purchasable amounts of goods by a unit of money. This is calculated by the following procedure. Let us denote the value of money as x. Then the following relationship holds: $px = 1$ Thus, we obtain $x = \frac{1}{p}$.
3 For a more detailed analysis, with which is dealt in this subsection, see Otaki (2015).
4 For rigorous derivations of Equations 2.13 and 2.16, see Otaki (2007, 2011)
5 Keynes (2013, p. 320) assert that '[t]here are therefore getting into the position, which is dangerous, of having property in legal tender instead of in real property. I think it is correct to say that in past history, every long-lived institution which has had its property in legal tender instead of real values has been ultimately ruined, because in the long run, the value of any legal tender always falls towards zero, If you are considering considerable periods of time.' Such assertion seems to be based on the discussion here in the sense that the technological progress unavoidably depreciates the value of money.
6 See Otaki and Tamai (2012) for more detail on the mathematical background.

References

Coase, Ronald H. (1937). The nature of the firm. *Economica, 4,* 1–27.
Fukuda, Akio (2010) The Era of 80 thousands New Residences ⇒ Busted Bubble ⇒ Towards recovery. Retrieved from http://www.jhf.go.jp/files/100055633.pdf#search='1994%E5%B9%B4%E3%81%AE%E3%83%9E%E3%83%B3%E3%82%B7%E3%83%A7%E3%83%B3%E3%81%AE%E5%B9%B3%E5%9D%87%E4%BE%A1%E6%A0%BC'

Keynes, J. M. (1936) *The General Theory of Employment, Interest and Money.* London: Macmillan.

Keynes, J. M. (2013) *Activities 1931–1939: World Crises and Policies in Britain and America.* In *The Collected Writings of John Maynard Keynes XXI,* Edited by D. Moggridge. Cambridge, UK: Cambridge University Press.

Otaki, M. (2007) The dynamically extended Keynesian cross and the welfare-improving fiscal policy. *Economics Letters*, Vol. 96, 23–29.

Otaki, M. (2011) A pure theory of aggregate price determination. *Theoretical Economics Letters,* Vol. 1, 122–128.

Otaki, M. (2015) *Keynesian Economics and Price Theory: Re-orientation of a Theory of Monetary Economy.* Tokyo: Springer.

Otaki, M. and Y. Tamai (2012) A microeconomic foundation for the Phillips curve under complete market without any price stickiness: a Keynesian view, *Theoretical Economics Letters, 2,* 482–486.

Research Institute of Immobile Assets (2013) *Suumo Journal.* http://suumo.jp/journal/2013/08/13/50160/

Sanyu System Appraisal (2013) Sanyu land price index: current land price movement in Tokyo metropolitan area. http://www.sanyu-appraisal.co.jp/res/pdf/25–6.pdf

3 Are the current Japanese economy and the Showa Depression alike?

3.1 Critiques to advocates of reflation

Some Japanese economists (e.g., Iwata 2004) argue that the combination of 'deflation' and high unemployment in the current Japanese economy is akin to the Showa Depression which exploded in 1930. The most prominent feature which characterizes the Showa Depression is the acute monetary contraction due to the gold standard system. Iwata (2004) allege that current Japanese economy and the Showa Depression are alike, and therefore, the emergent and unlimited monetary expansion is necessary to recover from the current stagnant economy. Such claim, amplified by baseless mass media assertions, is supported by numerous lay people in economics and economic history even fanatically.

However, their assertions are preposterous in the following two points.

(1) There is a decisive difference in the foreign exchange system, which advocates completely neglect. That is, the Japanese government adopted gold standard when the Great Depression diffused from the United States to Japan as the Showa Depression. However, current foreign exchange system is a flexible exchange rate system, which excludes the convertibility of the currency (JPY) into gold.

As discussed in detail in Section 3.2, we must emphasize that, in gold standard, current account imbalance directly provokes domestic monetary imbalance. This is because parities are fixed to gold, and thus, adjustment by a change of exchange rate is not feasible. However, a monetary autonomy is, in principle, established unrelated to current account imbalance in the flexible exchange rate system.

(2) The acute economic factor, which triggers the two economic stagnations, is quite different. The Showa Depression originated from the grievous monetary contraction caused by huge capital account deficits owing to the Great Depression in the United States. In this sense, the monetary incident dominates during the Showa Depression.

In contrast, current stagnation from the bust of the Bubble (1991) owes much real incidents. As exhibited in Tables 2.4 and 3.1, Japanese economy steadily grew until the1990s. That is, we must note that the aggregate demand management policy succeeded in mitigating depressive shocks adjacent to the busted bubble. Table 1.2 also suggests that such growth is mainly pulled by the large sum of fiscal expenditure financed by public deficits. As will be discussed in Tables 3.3 and 3.4, monetary contraction is scarcely observed.

Table 3.1 Japanese nominal GDP (trillion JPY)

1985	1990	1995	2000	2005	2010
33,1	45,4	50,1	50,2	51,6	49,3

Data Source: SNA Statistics (Cabinet Office).

Such evidence implies that the vicious cycle due to real incidents formed in 2.5 sets in motion especially around the turn of this century because additional governmental stimulation became challenging due to hardship in fiscal discipline.

To summarize, the current prolonged recession is triggered by real incidents. One is stagnant consumption owing to the pessimistic views on future income. The other is the leakage of effective demand to overseas such as the surge of foreign direct investment (FDI) seeking cheaper wages and foreign markets. As discussed in Chapters 1 and 2, these incidents become more prominent around the turn of the century and aggravated business conditions in the domestic economy.

Thus, in reality, origins of the two serious economic stagnations are quite different. Assertions of Iwata (2004) are no less than factitious. Moreover, they might contain some precarious political will, prompting inflation which is unduly incontrollable.

This chapter is organized as follows. Section 3.2 deals with the theory of gold standard, which was adopted in the Showa Depression, and analyzes how the system relates to the autonomy of monetary policy. In Section 3.3, the theory of current flexible exchange rate system is concisely reviewed from the same point of view as the gold standard. Based on these discussions and using actual data, we show that financial conditions are entirely different between these two economic stagnations. Section 3.5 asserts, referring to theories and facts from the sections above, that the advocate of the reckless monetary expansion as a remedy for the current prolonged stagnation is quite precarious when we recognize stringently the facts that the Japanese public debts surmount 12 trillion JPY (about twice her GDP) and that an artificially made-up inflation devastates the confidence of their values. Section 3.6 presents concluding remarks.

3.2 Mechanism of gold standard in actual

Gold standard decisively relies on *confidence* of gold in the sense defined in Section 2.3; that is, the belief that gold can be always exchanged for goods at some fixed ratio. This belief, in turn, implies that the price level is unrelated to amounts of gold that a country holds.

Such a belief stabilizes the domestic price level, but also, a country is forced to face a serious liquidity crunch when it experiences the current account deficit. Since the nominal exchange rate (the parity) is fixed to ensure the *confidence* of gold, a current account imbalance adjoins the outflow of gold from a deficit country to a surplus country.

Since the convertibility of a currency to gold is guaranteed, a liquidity crunch ensues. Such a crisis mitigates new investment opportunities and shrinks the governmental budget. Thus, differing from the flexible exchange rate system, where a change of the exchange rate cancels the international diffusion of business cycle at least to some extent, current account deficits directly downturn business cycle under gold standard.

While export-promoting policies are a kind of virtue under gold standard in the sense that this simultaneously expands the domestic credits, the significance of such policies is rather eroded under the flexible exchange rate, because currency provision is permitted to be isolated from the hoarded gold, and a substantial increase in export appreciates the exchange rate, and thus the non-negligible part of values of export is evaporated by such an appreciation. That is, advanced countries that are eager to promote their exports are still left in the era of gold standard, in which the autonomy of monetary policy was not permitted.

To summarize, the most prominent feature of gold standard is that there is no autonomy of monetary policy among the affiliates. The imbalance of balance of payments (current accounts plus capital accounts) necessarily adjoins the monetary expansion/contraction in domestic markets.

3.3   Ideal mechanism of gold standard: theory of specie flow

Gold standard originated from the combination of the purchasing power parity (PPP) and *disbelief* in the value of gold. The value of gold in terms of goods decreases proportionately with its volume. Furthermore, the domestic price of goods is determined so that it is equalized with the domestic price of foreign goods.

Let us represent the ratio of gold, which is necessary to purchase unit of goods, with k. That is,

$$\frac{M}{p} = k \tag{3.1}$$

M denotes the quantity of the fiducial money to gold, whereas p and p^* denote prices of goods in domestic and foreign markets, respectively. π is the fixed nominal exchange rate calculated from the parity of each currency.

Then, the purchasing power parity (PPP) theory asserts that

$$p = \pi p^* \tag{3.2}$$

That is, PPP is a kind of the arbitrage theory between the same kinds of goods. When the foreign price p^* falls, import from the foreign country advances, and thus p also falls because the aggregate supply of goods in the domestic market becomes abundant.

The foreign price decrease to λp^* ($0 < \lambda < 1$), the domestic price downs to λp by Equation 3.2. Since people disbelieve the value of gold, in conjunction with deficits in the balance of payment, we can calculate by Equation 3.1 that the hoarded gold (fiducial money) M outflows to overseas as much as

$$kp[1-\lambda]$$

Consequently, the exchange ratio of gold to the domestic goods is kept at k. Meanwhile, because the purchasing power of gold k is kept intact, the domestic business environment is isolated completely from the foreign price movement. Hence the business cycle is considered not to diffuse across countries. Gold standard has been regarded as a coherent international financial settlement measure, especially during the eighteenth century. This theory is also the backbone of Japanese advocates of gold standard (e.g., Junnosuke Inoue who was the Minister of Finance in the Hamaguchi cabinet which enacted return to gold standard).

Nonetheless, the cruelty of gold standard becomes prominent around the turn of the twentieth century. As discussed in Section 3.2, the overseas downturn of business exacerbates the deficits of balance of payment and chokes the monetary conditions in the domestic economy. This triggers a serious depression also in the domestic economy. As such, subtle economists abandoned "the theory of specie flow."[1]

The theory of specie flow contains a serious contradiction. That is, the theory assumes the confidence of gold in international economy because gold is the only measure available and/or reliable for international settlement. However, in the domestic economy, the intrinsic value of gold is disbelieved, and that decreases proportionately with the hoarded volume.

In reality, people were confident of the value of gold under gold standard, and thereby international business cycle diffusion becoming serious.

3.4   Mechanism of the flexible exchange rate system with a key currency

The current international settlement is based on the flexible exchange rate system that does not presume the convertibility of currencies to gold. Among currencies, USD plays a prominent role: the key currency. Most international financial transactions are settled in terms of USD. This is considered to reflex the world economy's confidence of the strength of economic potentialities of the United States. In this sense, USD is the substitute for gold in pre-war era, although its intrinsic value varies via the change of exchange rates along with economic conditions.

Such regime can be regarded as a worldwide implicit insurance system against sovereign risks.[2] Many countries regard USD as an insurance security against their own sovereign risks endorsed by the overwhelming industrial potential of the United States. This enables USD to circulate as an international currency, that is, key currency.

Hence, the United States can enjoy huge amounts of seigniorage as the insurance fee. Such seigniorage appears as deficits of the current account because public debts of the United States hoarded overseas are equivalent to claims of USD.

Thus, the United States is the only country implicitly permitted to sustain current account deficits.

This, in turn, implies that the rest of countries who are affiliates of USD currency area record the surplus in their current account. This can be regarded as an implicit insurance fee paid for using USD.

Although it is quite difficult to estimate how much the Japanese economy tributes such fee, Table 3.2 reveals that its current account surplus per GDP is around 1 to 2 per cent. (Note that the value is exceptionally high from 1985 to 1989.) According to our theory, this implies that Japanese purchase insurance securities, whose name is USD, against her sovereign risks with 2 per cent risk premium at most.[3] It seems that such premium is not so exorbitant from the intrinsic vulnerability of Japanese economy.[4]

Eliminating such implicit and unvaried insurance fee, we can regard that the current account of the Japanese economy is almost equilibrated from the early 1980s and thereafter. On the other hand, as illustrated by Figure 3.1, there is a prominent appreciation trend in the nominal exchange rate of JPY relative to USD.

This fact implies that, *ceteris paribus,* the export of Japan exceed its import. When the exchange rate appreciates, foreign prices of exported goods become

Table 3.2 Japanese current account surplus per GDP (%)

1980–1984	1985–1989	1990–1994	1995–1999	2000–2004	2005–2009
0.9	2.8	1.8	1.2	1.4	0.9

Data Source: SNA Statistics (Cabinet Office).

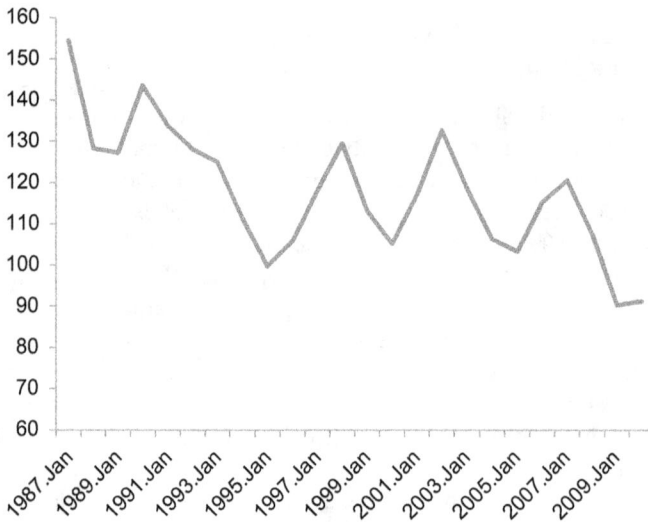

Figure 3.1 The exchange rate

dear, and sales are thwarted. Imported goods to the domestic economy become cheap and extend their sales. Thus, the current account moves towards equilibrium. This is the fundamental adjustment process embedded within the flexible exchange rate system with a key currency.[5]

Accordingly, differing from gold standard, the domestic monetary policy is never constrained by the imbalance of current account. Even though the United States experiences serious current account deficits, there is no need for the contractionary monetary policy in the flexible exchange rate system. Japan is also permitted to pursuit the extremely easy monetary policy despite of its descending current surplus. Thus, the vital feature in the flexible exchange rate system with a key currency is that monetary policy of each country is emancipated from the constraint of its balance of payment.

3.5 Actual difference between the current stagnation and the Showa Depression

The typical difference between the current prolonged stagnation and the Showa Depression appears in money supply. The Showa Depression in conjunction with the rapid and huge capital account deficit, the Japanese government was forced to face outflow of fiducial currency and to contract money supply as illustrated by Figure 3.2. As compared with 1929 (the year before the Depression), the fiducial currency decreased to 30 per cent in 1934 (Ministry of Finance [1947–1964]).[6]

This violent monetary contraction concentrated in 1930 and 1931 tightened the lending conditions, especially to fabric industries. Banks urged to recall their money from such industries, and the entrepreneurs were forced to sell their products at no breathing margins for repayments. Most small and fragile fabric firms (especially belonging to silk industry) bankrupted, or even if not so, they

Figure 3.2 The stock of fiducial currency

drastically slashed employee's wages, and many workers were fired. Thus, the depression was deepened.

We must note that the Japanese economy suffered serious current account deficits during several years ahead of the abolishment of embargo (January 1930). Such deficits are due to expansionary fiscal policies that aimed to construct new infrastructures (rail roads, urban planning, subsidies for nurturing heavy industries, and etc.). That is, it is foreseeable that rejoining gold standard was genetically infeasible for Japan judging from the incessant current account deficits adjacent to huge fiscal deficits.

In this sense, the rejoining at the excessively high parity only triggered the tremendous outflow of the fiducial currency. Every subtle speculator foresaw the embargo in the near future (December 1931) at the very beginning of return to gold standard. They purchased huge amounts of USD in exchange for fiducial currency, and thus severe domestic monetary contraction occurred.

To summarize, the most prominent feature of the Showa Depression is the appalling domestic monetary contraction owing to the unreasonable return to gold standard. Such contraction choked bank loans especially towards small and fragile firms in the fabric industry. Facing the hardship, these entrepreneurs were forced to sell their products at damping prices, cut wages and fire some parts of their employees. Consequently, prominent deflation progressed as illustrated by Figure 3.3.

Contrary to the protagonist during the Showa Depression, current prolonged stagnation is characterized by the historical easy monetary policy. Table 3.3 shows the increase rate of the monetary base per annum accelerates throughout

Figure 3.3 Consumer Price Index

Table 3.3 Averaged increase rate of monetary base per annum (%)

1991–1999	2000–2009	2010–2013
3.1	5.2	15.0

Data Source: The Bank of Japan.

post-Bubble Era.[7] Such an arbitrary policy has been infeasible until the central bank becomes free from the imbalance of the current account under the flexible exchange rate system with the key currency. That is, as discussed in the previous section, the current account is located around the equilibrium autonomously, when we count the implicit insurance fee charged by the key currency country (i.e., United States).

To summarize, circumstances that prescribe the both recessions are quite different: the Showa Depression originated from the acute monetary contraction brought about by gold standard. The current prolonged stagnation can be regarded unrelated to the monetary conditions because financial expansion continues during almost a quarter of a century. The analyses in Iwata (2004) are preposterous in the sense that they entirely confuse the crucial differences in foreign exchange rate systems. This evidence also implies that there is a limit in monetary policy as a measure for boosting the economy under the flexible exchange rate system.[8]

3.6 The precariousness of Iwata's assertion: there is no theory in which inflation advances business upturn

The assertion of Iwata (2004) is quite naïve and provocative. By exemplifying the Showa Depression, they allege that the recent negligible deflation since around 2010 can be cured by some aggressive expansionary monetary policy. As discussed in 2.3.1, they are fanatic captives in the quantity theory of money.

More seriously, they insist the opposite causality existing between business upturn and inflation. That is, they propagate that the acceleration of inflation is able to upturn business.

As discussed in 3.2.4 in more detail, the true causality is converse: an upturn in business triggers the progress of labor productivity via stabilizing employees' daily life. This is because the progress proportionately increases the nominal wage. Since the raised wage makes breathing space for employees, employers can also provide dear goods. This implies the acceleration of inflation. That is, the true causality is as follows.

Business upturn ⇒ Progress of labor productivity
⇒ Increase in nominal wage ⇒ Acceleration of inflation

Whenever money is in disbelief and expectations on the future value of money are fluttered by some exorbitant monetary policy, the acceleration of inflation advances. In such a case, the purchasing power of whole nominal assets declines along with the increase in the growth of money supply, and hence this suppresses effective demand. As a result, it is certain that the most grievous stagflation, in which stagnation and high inflation rate coexist, will emerge. This can be expressed by the following chart.

Exorbitant expansionary monetary policy ⇒ Acceleration of inflation
⇒ Decrease in the purchasing power of nominal assets
⇒ Suppression of effective demand ⇒ Grievous stagflation

This stagflation is quite harmful for most citizens in the following two senses. First, it deprives of the purchasing power of monetary assets by inflation tax as discussed in 2.2. Such incomes are transferred implicitly to owners of stocks and land where returns are not fixed in terms of money. This will rescue holders of such assets who are considered to be heavily indebted by the bust of the Bubble.

When we consider the exorbitant public debt stock, which is mainly held by banks, it is certain that such inflation will threaten the business management of these financial intermediaries. That is, there possibly emerges a new financial crisis. In this sense, we must eschew any excessive expansionary monetary policy.

Second, unemployment that would increase due to a decrease in the purchasing power of nominal assets also aggravates the disparity in income distribution. Thus, no one, except for the stock/land owners, can be better off by an exorbitant monetary policy. Iwata's assertion is a symbol of the despotic capitalism defined in 1.3.

3.7   Concluding remarks

In this chapter, we have considered the validity of Iwata's (2004) assertion that the current prolonged stagnation and the Showa Depression are alike, and a radical monetary policy is indispensable for recovery of the Japanese economy. Obtained results are as follows.

1. The current stagnation that originated from the bust of the Bubble around the early 1990s is caused by economic incidents quite different from those in the Showa Depression. Especially, we must note that the foreign exchange system entirely differs between both stagnations. We are now standing on the flexible exchange rate system with the key currency. In contrast to this, the Showa Depression was triggered under gold standard. In this sense, Iwata's (2004) assertion is based on the spurious inspection.
2. The Showa Depression is triggered by the acute monetary contraction along with the grievous downturn in exports towards the United States, which was amidst the Great Depression. Under gold standard, prominent deficits in the balance of payment immediately adjoin a severe monetary contraction because large amounts of fiducial currency outflow to overseas.

    It is evident that such a situation is quite different from the extremely easy money regime throughout the current prolonged stagnation under the flexible exchange rate with the key currency, in which domestic monetary policy can be free from imbalance of the balance of payment. In this sense, Iwata's (2004) assertion is preposterous.

3. The inflation-prompting policy recommendation is quite precarious, when we consider exorbitant stock of the public debt. If the confidence of money is fluttered by such a reckless monetary policy, it is certain that inflation is accelerated. Nevertheless, it is also inevitable that the value of the public debt will be devastated. The bust of the value of the public debt surely aggravates the business of financial intermediaries that hoard most part of these assets. This implies that there is a serious precariousness that the reckless inflation-prompting monetary policy triggers a financial crisis in the Japanese economy, which possibly by far exceeds the bust of the Bubble in the early 1990s.

Notes

1 Keynes (2013) vividly depicts how he tackled this vital problem. We must note that, unlike Japan, the United Kingdom was the key currency country until the outbreak of the World War II, and thus, it faced more complex problems. Alfred Marshall said in his letter to Keynes (pp. 162–163), 'As years go on it seems to become even clear that there ought to be an international currency; and that the – in itself foolish – superstition that gold is the "natural" representation of value has done excellent service. I have appointed myself amateur currency-mediciner; but I cannot give myself even a tolerably good testimonial in that capacity.' However, nowadays (only after about 90 years from the Marshall's letter being written), there are few who are confident in the value of gold. Thus, what people are confident in as the standard of value is transferable, especially under the current rapid financial innovation.
2 See Otaki (2012, 2013) for more details on the function of the flexible exchange rate system under a key currency.
3 Note that Japan is scarcely endowed with natural resources, especially crude oil and minerals and that the transaction of these resources is almost settled in terms of USD.
4 We must note that our key-currency theory, which is an application of insurance theory to international macroeconomics, presumes that the key-currency country should have an overwhelming industrial power and the soundness of the economy to be able to cover insurances.
5 There is an authorized theory which emphasizes that the disparity between interest rates crucially affects the movement of the exchange rate unrelated to the current account (Fleming 1962, Mundell 1963). That is, high-interest country experiences the appreciation of its exchange rate because investors find advantageous opportunity in such a country. They purchase its currency for the investment, and thus the exchange rate appreciates. Consequently,

$$i_t = i_t^* + \frac{\pi_{t+1} - \pi_t}{\pi_t}$$

holds. i_t is the domestic short-term interest rate. i_t^* is the foreign short term interest rate, and π is the nominal exchange rate. The left-hand side of the above equation is the rate of return from the domestic asset, and the right-hand side is that from the foreign asset. The above equation implies that the nominal exchange is determined at the level which the excess return from the foreign investment is vanished. However, as depicted by Table 3.4, it is inconceivable to assume that such uncovered interest parity holds.

Table 3.4 Excess return of the foreign asset, Japanese call rate, and the risk premium (%)

	1985–1989	1990–1994	1995–1999	2000–2004	2005–2009
Excess Return	12.2	6.5	5.3	1.4	4.6
Japanese Call Rate	4.89	4.94	0.43	0.03	0.17
Risk Premium	2.49	1.31	12.3	46.6	27.0

Data Source: Exchange Rate and Japanese Call Rate (The Bank of Japan Federal Funds Rate; New York Federal Reserve Bank).

That is, the appreciation of JPY to USD is never able to attribute to the interest disparity between the two countries. The excess return to the short term dollar asset is significantly positive throughout sample periods. In addition, the risk premium for the dollar asset, which is defined by the ratio of the excess return to the Japanese call rate has been extremely higher since the late 1990s.

Accordingly, these facts imply that the movement of the nominal exchange rate cannot be explained by the disparity of the interest rates between Japan and the United States.

6 It seems curious that the current accounts of 1930 and 1931 only recorded slight deficits despite of the flux of the fiducial currency (Miwa 2011, p. 117). However, this suggests that the capital accounts experienced huge amount of surplus, which was canceled by the corresponding decrease in the foreign reserve.

7 In the early 1990s, a contractive monetary policy was adopted. The monetary base contracts by −1.5 per cent during 1992 and −3.1 per cent during 1993, respectively. Such policies aimed to extinguish the Bubble. Excluding these data, we obtain that the average increase rate of the monetary base during the 1990s is 5.2 per cent per annum.

8 It is quite precarious that the average increase rate of monetary base exploded up to 32.8 per cent per annum during 2013, when Iwata become the vice president of BOJ and that the baseless political applause for 'Abenomics' is boosted via mass media.

References

Fleming, J. M. (1962) Domestic fiscal policies under fixed and floating exchange rates. IMF Staff Papers, 9.

Iwata, K. (eds.) (2004) *A Study on the Showa Depression* (in Japanese) [Showa Kyoko no Kenkyu]. Tokyo: Toyo Keizai Shinpo-sha.

Keynes, J.M. (2013) *Activities 1931–1939: World Crises and Policies in Britain and America. The Collected Writings of John Maynard Keynes XXI,* Edited by D. Moggridge. Cambridge, UK: Cambridge University Press.

Ministry of Finance (1947–1964). *The Fiscal History of Showa: Prewar Era* (in Japanese) [Showa Zaisei Shi: Senzen-hen]. Tokyo: Toyo Keizai Shinpo-sha.

Miwa, R. (2011) *An Outline of Japanese Economic History since the 1850s* (in Japanese) [Gaisetsu Nihon Keizai-shi: Kingendai]. 3rd edition. Tokyo: University of Tokyo Press.

Mundel, R.A. (1963) Capital mobility and stabilization policy under fixed and flexible exchange rates. *Canadian Journal of Economics and Political Science, 29,* 475–485.

Otaki, M. (2012) A Keynesian model of a small open economy under a flexible exchange rate. *Theoretical Economics Letters, 2,* 278–282.

Otaki, M. (2013) How a key currency functions as an international liquidity provision and insurance system. *Theoretical Economics Letters, 3,* 43–47.

4 'Abenomics' in reality

4.1 The overview of Abenomics

This chapter deals with so-called Abenomics, a nexus of the radical stimulating economic policies that have been enhanced by the 2nd Abe cabinet since the end of 2012. Abenomics comprises the following three economic policies:

I.   The exorbitant expansionary monetary policy (Ijigen Kinnyu Seisaku: Quantitative Easing policy of Japanese version)
II. The fiscal expansion despite the crisis of the public debt confidence
III. The growth-enhancing strategy (GES: Seicho Senryaku) that opens the opportunity for unrestricted wage cutting

In this chapter, Policy I is critically examined, and the results from the previous chapters are discussed. This is partly because the consequences of Policy II are inseparable from those of Policy I in the sense that enlarged budget deficits directly connect to the explosion of nominal assets, partly because there is no substantial information about the contents of Policy III, and we can regard this merely as the extension of the Structural Reformation by the Koizumi cabinets.

To summarize, Abenomics does not contain anything essentially new compared with the policies during the Structural Reformation Era that were analyzed in Chapter 1. This nexus of the policies comprises a hodgepodge of textbook-like Keynesian policy proposal (Policy I and II) and neoclassical policy measures that were called the *supply-side economics* in Reaganomics era during the mid-1980s (Policy III). The above policy measures I and II are based on the naïve and ineffective IS/LM analysis and are powerless when an economy encounters a serious fiscal crisis as contemporary Japanese economy does.

It will be shown that the exorbitant expansionary monetary policy does not have any relationship with the transitory boom of the stock market from 2013 and that such a policy hinders economic growth conversely and accelerates disinflation. That is, the glut of base money provoked by the exorbitant expansionary monetary policy requires a higher return for money in itself to equilibrate the market. Since Japanese economy faces the substantially zero-interest policy, and thus the rate of return for money is substantively equal to the inverse of the inflation rate, disinflation is ensued by the exponential increase in the base money. Disinflation heightens the opportunity cost for capital investment for progressing labor productivity, and thus, this becomes an obstacle for enhancing economic growth against the policy makers' will.[1] We dub this phenomenon the *asset crowding out*.

In addition, it will be clarified that the boom in the Japanese stock market during 2013 does not originate from the exorbitant expansionary monetary policy. There were huge inflows from the foreign sector that amounted about 1.5 trillion yen for purchasing the Japanese stocks during 2013. Although a favorable evaluation to the abdication of the cabinet of the Democratic Party should be taken into the consideration, one must note that the United States has suffered from a serious fiscal crisis since 2011. It is never denied that the disbelief in the value of dollar triggered such huge inflows into the Japanese stock market. In this sense, the boom in the stock market only coincided with the inauguration of Shinzo Abe. That is, one must recognize that the domestic political hardship in the United States relates to the boom in the stock market quite significantly.

Nevertheless, the voluminous stock purchased by foreign investors, ceteris paribus, would appreciate the nominal exchange rage. However, Japan experiences a prominent depreciation of the nominal exchange rate in the same period. Thus, there should be another economic incident that dominates the appreciation effect caused by the boom in the stock market. This is the effect ipso fact of the exorbitant expansionary monetary policy. Although major part of money supplied via the massive open market operation stays within the excess reserves of city banks at Bank of Japan (BOJ), the residual part is directly invested into foreign securities such as Treasury Bills. Indirectly, the Japanese banks also use their excess reserves as collaterals for the foreign security investment. As such, there is a strong tendency to induce the depreciation of yen. The amount of borrowed securities from foreign investors during 2013 is estimated 20 trillion yen. This by far exceeds the inflow of the purchase of Japanese stocks by foreign investors. Accordingly, the exorbitant expansionary monetary policy (the extra-dimensional monetary policy) is the accurate cause of the recent depreciation of yen.

To summarize, the exorbitant expansionary monetary policy acutely depreciates the nominal exchange rate, while it is unconceivable that such policy relates to the boom in the stock market.

4.2   The consequences of the exorbitant expansionary monetary policy

4.2.1   *Reconstructing the effective demand theory*

This subsection reconstructs the effective demand theory proposed by Keynes (1936) to explain the situation in which current Japanese economy is entrapped. The prominent shortcoming of the Keynes' effective demand theory is that his theory neglects the direct contribution of the quantity of money to effective demand. In the simplest form, the effective demand theory advocates that real gross domestic product (GDP) is determined at the level where aggregate savings, which are proportional to the real GDP, are equal to the sum of aggregate capital investments and government expenditures.

However, one must note that there is another component of effective demand at least in a sufficiently long-time horizon where economic growth becomes effective: the stock of money. The incumbent money holders spend almost all his or her money after his or her retirement, and thus the real stock of money is also a constituent of effective demand in the long run. Keynes (1936) neglects this important effect since his concern is concentrated within the short-run movement of an economy. The effect of nominal assets such as public debt on effective demand is similar to the one described in this discussion.

One may argue that the consumption of incumbent money holders is the same amount of savings of a new holder simultaneously, and hence there might be no contribution to effective demand. Nevertheless, it must be emphasized that aggregate savings of new money holders crucially depend on their aggregate incomes, while incumbents' consumption is inelastic to any economic variable if they have no inheritance motive. Accordingly, real incomes (real GDP) can be never invariant in conjunction with a change of the real cash balance. In addition, such direct effect of the real cash balance to effective demand should rigorously be discriminated from the somewhat ad hoc and indirect effect where an increase in money stock lowers the rate of interest and stimulates capital investment (i.e., the liquidity preference theory).

Since the exorbitant expansionary monetary policy requires an economy with a higher rate of return for money (i.e., the inverse of the inflation rate) for clearing the goods market, such policy improves aggregate savings and hinders (human) capital investment as long as real GDP (per capita) is kept intact. Thus, under some realistic conditions, the exorbitant expansionary monetary policy with the zero interest rate policy hinders economic growth conversely as is observed in current Japanese economy.

Finally, it should be highlighted that this discussion presumes that the exorbitant expansionary monetary policy does not collapse the confidence in money as defined in Chapter 2. If this policy impairs such a cornerstone of social stability, it provokes fearful hyperinflation or the default of the public debt.

4.2.2   Time preference and monetary policy

As discussed in Chapter 2, the slowdown in the progress of labor productivity is closely connected to the prominent disinflation of Japanese economy. However, that discussion excludes effects of human capital accumulation process within a firm. This subsection shows that the exorbitant expansionary monetary policy aggravates labor productivity progress and becomes an obstacle for economic growth.

The intuitive formulation of the theory is as follows. There are two markets in an economy: goods market and money market. One of these is not independent according to Walras' law. The analysis is concentrated to money market, of which equilibrium condition is depicted as

$$s\tilde{y} - \iota(\pi) = m \tag{4.1}$$

where s is the marginal propensity to saving, and $\tilde{y}$ is real National Domestic Product (NDP) per capita. $\iota(\pi)$ is the human capital investment per capita. m denotes the total real money supply per capita. π is the inflation rate (the inverse of the rate of return for money). Since an increase in the inflation rate π reduces the opportunity cost of capital investment, the investment function $\iota(\pi)$ is an increasing function of π. Thus, Equation 4.1 is illustrated by the upward sloping curve DD in Figure 4.1. One must note that the slope of curve DD becomes flatter together with a decreasing in the value of s. This is due to the higher value of the fiscal multiplier.

Equation 4.1 represents the double aspects of the role of money. For a new money holder, money is a measure for saving that amounts to $s\tilde{y} - \iota(\pi)$. The other aspect of money is the inelastic consumption demand of an incumbent money holder that amounts to m. Equation 4.1 implies that the demand and supply for money must be equilibrated. This equation corresponds to the modified aggregated demand function.

The other condition required for describing an economy is the aggregate supply function that corresponds to the *fundamental equation* introduced in Chapter 2. Let's assume that the production of the representative firm follows the shape to be postulated in Chapter 6, that is,

$$Y_t = F\left(\Psi\left(k_t, L_{t-1}^S\right), L_t\right) \tag{4.2}$$

where Y_t is the total output during period t, and k_t is the deployed physical capital. L_{t-1}^S and L_t denote the existing skilled worker measured by an efficiency unit

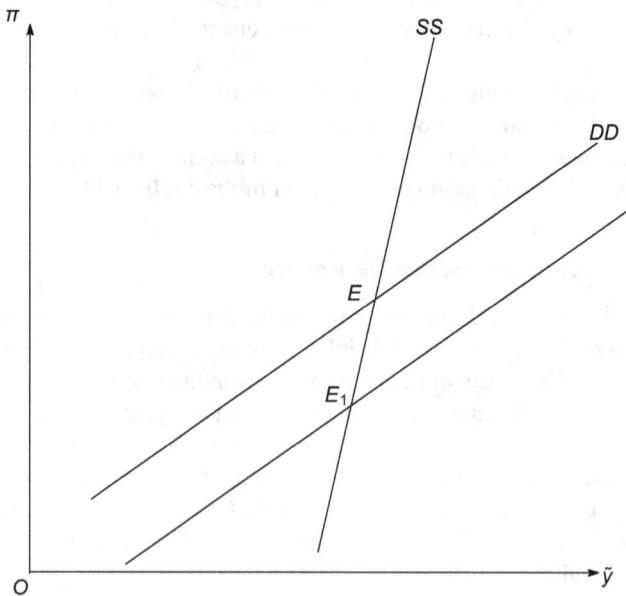

Figure 4.1 Asset crowding out

and the total employer including unskilled labor force, respectively. Under perfect competition, the profit-maximization condition in the short run requires

$$\frac{\partial}{\partial k} F\left(\Psi\left(\frac{k_t}{L_t}, \frac{L_{t-1}^S}{L_t}\right), 1\right) = 1 \tag{4.3}$$

and

$$F\left(\Psi\left(\frac{k_t^*}{L_t^*}, \frac{L_{t-1}^S}{L_t^*}\right), 1\right) - \frac{\partial}{\partial\left[L_{t-1}^S / L_t\right]} F\left(\Psi\left(\frac{k_t^*}{L_t^*}, \frac{L_{t-1}^S}{L_t^*}\right), 1\right) \cdot \frac{L_{t-1}^S}{L_t^*} = w_t^R \tag{4.4}$$

Equation 4.3 implies that the marginal product of physical capital must be equal to its unit price, and thus, the unit effective physical capital, which embodies workers' skill $\frac{\Psi}{L_t}$ takes a constant value over time. Equation 4.4 represents the condition that the marginal product of unskilled worker must be equalized to its marginal cost: the real reservation wage, w_t^R.

After differentiating both sides of Equation 4.4 by taking the result of Equation 4.3 into consideration, we obtain

$$-\frac{\partial^2 F}{\partial\left[L_{t-1}^S / L_t\right]^2} \Big|_{\substack{k_t = k_t^* \\ L_t = L_t^*}} \cdot \frac{L_{t-1}^S}{L_t^*} \cdot d\frac{L_{t-1}^S}{L_t^*} = dw_t^R \tag{4.5}$$

Thus, it is clear that the demand for unskilled workers is a decreasing function of the real reservation wage. Furthermore, combining Equation 4.5 with 4.4, it can be induced that real NDP per capita $\tilde{y}$ satisfies the following relationship:

$$\tilde{y} \equiv F\left(\Psi\left(\frac{k_t^*}{L_t^*}, \frac{L_{t-1}^S}{L_t^*}\right), 1\right) - \frac{k_t^*}{L_t^*}$$

$$\Rightarrow d\tilde{y} = -\frac{\partial}{\partial\left[L_{t-1}^S / L_t\right]} F\left(\Psi\left(\frac{k_t}{L_t}, \frac{L_{t-1}^S}{L_t}\right), 1\right) \Big|_{\substack{k_t = k_t^* \\ L_t = L_t^*}} \cdot \frac{L_{t-1}^S}{\left[L_t^*\right]^2} dL_t^*. \tag{4.6}$$

Equation 4.6 implies that, in conjunction with an increase in the employment of unskilled worker, real NDP per capita decreases because of the decline of labor productivity. Therefore, one can ascertain that the following causality emerges:[2]

$$w_t^R \uparrow \Rightarrow L_t^* \downarrow \Rightarrow \tilde{y} \uparrow$$

Thus, real NDP per capita $\tilde{y}$ is an increasing function of the real reservation wage, w_t^R that is also an increasing function of the inflation rate, π. Consequently, we get that

$$\tilde{y} = y\big(w(\pi : s)\big), y' > 0 \tag{4.7}$$

Accordingly, the aggregate supply function in Equation 4.7 is upward sloping as illustrated by curve SS in Figure 4.1. It should be noted that Equation 4.7 is also a variant of the fundamental equation in case that the production functions is subject to decreasing return to scale.

Curve SS becomes more inelastic to the change of the inflation rate along with a decrease in the marginal propensity to saving, s. This is because a lower value of s implies that an individual is less concerned with future consumption than with current consumption, and hence he or she suffers less from the acceleration of inflation (Theoretically, those who have a low time preference rate record a lower marginal propensity to saving, s).[3] This implies that a larger change in the inflation rate should be associated with the adjustment of employment level and real NDP per capita. In subsequent analysis, let be assumed that individual prefer current consumption to future consumption and s takes the value small enough that the slope of curve SS is steeper than that of curve DD.

The equilibrium of an economy is achieved at the intersection E of curves DD and SS in Figure 4.1. Let the monetary asset, which might include public debts, be issued additionally, and thus the value of m increases. This shifts curve DD to the right side because real NDP per capita $\tilde{y}$ increases by the multiplier effect as long as the inflation rate π is kept intact. Thus, the economy moves from point E to E_1. The coexistence of disinflation and stagnation are prominent as such.[4] This theoretical analysis is not inconsistent with characteristics of Japanese economy under the exorbitant expansionary monetary policy and the huge accumulation of public debts.

The dominant causality, which provokes such grievous situations, is the *asset crowding out*. The exorbitant growth of monetary assets requires a higher rate of return to them for equilibrating the good/money market. Under zero-interest policy, such an adjustment inevitably yields the disinflation (note that disinflation is equivalent to an increase in the rate of return of money). Since disinflation (possibly including deflation) heightens the opportunity cost for (human) capital investment, the *asset crowding out*, which means that the accumulation of an asset is hindered by an increase in the rate of return of alternative assets, makes the economic growth rate decrease.

In addition, since disinflation lowers the cost of living, the nominal reservation wage, which is the minimum required wage to incentivize workers, is lowered. This might be one of the causes of continual nominal wages' downturn in Japanese economy. To sum up, there is a fatal inconsistency between the measures of Abenomics. As discussed above, the mechanism of economic growth becomes dysfunctional by Policies I and II described in Section 4.1 that aim to stimulate effective demand. This evidently contradicts the supply-side growth enhancing Policy III.

4.2.3   Some empirical evidence

Aside from biased and incautious information to much of which Japanese mass media should owe their responsibility, one can easily confirm that the exorbitant expansionary monetary policy never succeed in accelerating inflation. Figure 4.2 illustrates the time series of the Consumer Price Index (CPI: Ministry of Internal Affairs and Communications) that excludes foods and energies.[5] The figure suggests that disinflation (deflation) still continues despite the exorbitant expansionary monetary policy.

Figures 4.3 and 4.4 are the time series of the stocks of the monetary base and the widely defined liquidity (Kogi Rydosei), both of which includes the reserve of financial intermediary and public debts.

There are exorbitant increases in money of both concepts. The monetary base soars from 14 to 20 trillion yen during 2013. The widely defined liquidity jumps from 1460 to 1530 trillion yen. Regardless of the huge and incessant market

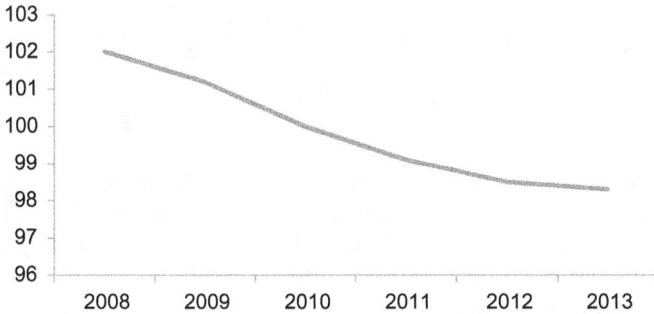

Figure 4.2 Consumer Price Index (excluding foods and energy)

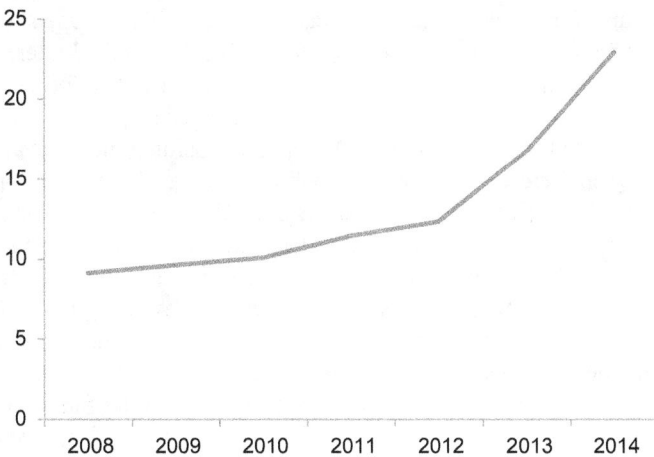

Figure 4.3 Monetary base (BOJ: trillion yen)

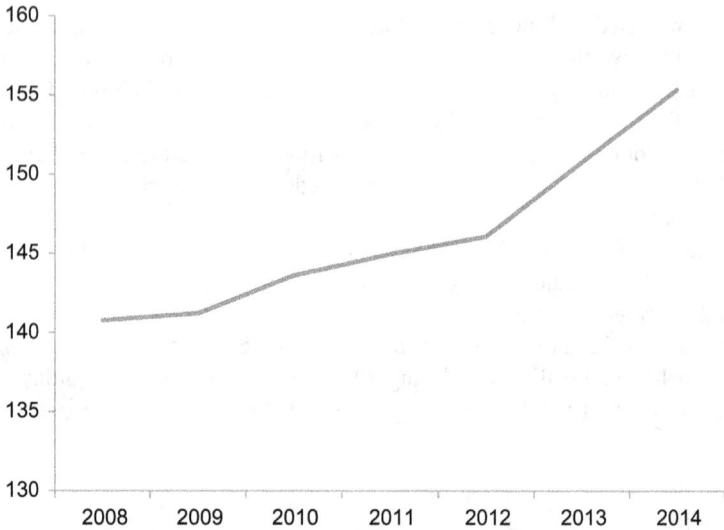

Figure 4.4 Widely defined liquidity (BOJ: trillion yen)

operations for providing monetary base in exchange for public debts, one must note that the increment of the widely defined liquidity exceeds that of the monetary base. This fact implies that although the exorbitant expansionary monetary policy is effective in the sense that this grievously enlarges the stock of nominal assets, the policy slightly affects the price level as such. This economic condition surrounding Japan is unable to understand based on the naïve quantity theory of money that many economists, who are intoxicated with populism, rest on.

The *asset crowding out* is a persuasive hypothesis that explains the advance of disinflation under the exorbitant expansionary monetary policy. One should realize that disinflation has the same effect as the sag of the nominal interest rate in the sense that both make money hoarding more fascinating. The former ipso facto empowers the purchasing power of money. The latter reduces the income accrued from securities, and thus, indirectly, makes money hoarding more advantageous. Under the ongoing zero-interest policy, by definition, the additional monetary assets cannot be absorbed by a change in the interest rate. Consequently, it is unavoidable that the exorbitant expansionary monetary policy accelerates disinflation.

The *asset crowding out* hypothesis also succeeds in elucidating one of the crucial reasons why the nominal wages in Japan were oppressed from the beginning of this century when the accumulation of nominal assets, which are mostly comprised by public debts, was prominent. As discussed in 2.3.2, the nominal wage W depends not only on the current price level p_t, but also the future price level p_{t+1}. That is,

$$W_t = W\left(p_t, p_{t+1}\right) \tag{4.8}$$

Current price is determined at the level, where the marginal productivity of labor is equalized to the unit labor cost, thus having

$$p_t = \frac{W(p_t, p_{t+1})}{\gamma(L_t)}, \gamma'(L_t) < 0 \qquad (4.9)$$

where γ is the marginal productivity of labor productivity and is a decreasing function of the total employment level, L_t. This is because the short-run production function is decreasing return to scale subject to the exiting skilled labor force. Insofar as the nominal wage W increases with the price levels (p_t, p_{t+1}) proportionately, Equation 4.9 is transformed into

$$W(p_t, p_{t+1}) = \gamma(L_t) p_t \Leftrightarrow \frac{W(p_t, p_{t+1})}{p_t} = W(1, \pi_{t+1}) = \gamma(L_t) \qquad (4.10)$$

Equation 4.10, which corresponds to the *fundamental equation* in case of decreasing marginal labor productivity, is illustrated in Figure 4.5.

Curve WW depicts the relationship between the real wage, $\frac{W(p_t, p_{t+1})}{p_t}$, and the total employment level, L_t. The horizontal curve shifts downwards when the inflation rate decreases, because disinflation, ceteris paribus, improves workers' well-being, and ensues the fierce competition among workers unless full employment is achieved. Curve LL corresponds to the marginal product of the total employment,

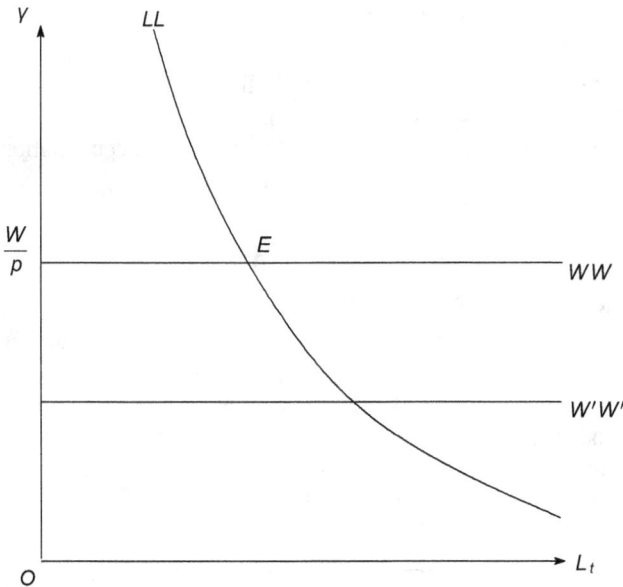

Figure 4.5 Disinflation and the marginal productivity of labor

and is downward sloping. This is because the marginal productivity of labor stagnates owing to the scarcity of skilled labor force together with the improvement of the total employment level, L_t.

The solution of the right Equation in 4.10 is depicted by point E. That implies that the optimal total employment level is determined at the point where the marginal product of labor is equalized to the real wage. Whenever disinflationary rational expectations prevail, curve WW moves downwards such as curve $W'W'$. Thus, labor productivity (also in the marginal product of labor) stagnates in conjunction with the improvement of the total employment level. In addition, the left Equation in 4.10 depicts that, if people are confident in the current value of money, and p_t is not affected by a change of γ, the nominal wage W is also reduced.

Intuitively, the provoked disinflationary rational expectations by the expansionary monetary policy trigger the ceaseless wage reduction and stagnates the progress of labor productivity. This comes from the fact that only low-quality labor forces are employable by a lower wage. The output price sags in accordance with a reduction in the nominal wage. This is the consistent movement of price with the phenomenon dubbed as the *asset crowding out*. As such, the following chart can be obtained concerning the relationship between the exorbitant expansionary policy, disinflation and the nominal wage:

Exorbitant Expansionary Monetary Policy $\Rightarrow$ Asset Crowding Out
$\Rightarrow$ Disinflation $\Rightarrow$ Nominal Wage Reduction $\Rightarrow$ Stagnation in Labor Productivity

In addition, one must note that, as apparent from Equation 4.1, the progress of dexterity is retarded by the exorbitant expansionary monetary policy because such a policy brings about substantial dear money via disinflation. Accordingly, economic growth is estimated to be lower than the above chart suggests. In other words, in conjunction with the economic hollowing brought by the excessive foreign direct investment (FDI) as will be analyzed in Chapter 6, the exorbitant monetary policy annihilates the genetic mechanism of the accumulation of human capital that has been embedded in Japanese economy.

4.3   The fuss in the stock market and Abenomics[6]

The previous section revealed that the exorbitant expansionary monetary policy conversely hinders domestic economic growth. However, such an assertion might perplex those who believe that the current boom in the stock market owes much to Abenomics. Nevertheless, as discussed above, the upturn of CPI is spurious in the sense that almost all this upturn attributes to the depreciation of the nominal exchange rate that is harmful for current Japanese economy. This is because factories of the manufacturing industries have moved overseas due to excessive FDI, and most of their profits are not remitted to domestic economy. Hence, the depreciation of yen only impoverishes import good industries. The prominent trade balance deficit and income account surplus in current Japanese economy are one of powerful evidences of this discussion. Accordingly, one

Table 4.1 The fiscal crisis in the United States

November 2008	QE1 (Quantitative Easing 1) was enacted by June 2010.
November 2010	QE2 by June 2011. FRB decided to buy the long-term public debt that amounts 75 billion dollar per month.
May 2011	The debt of the federal government reached its ceiling. The public debt problem was widely revealed.
August 2011	The Senate endorsed to lift the limit of public debt. Moody's and S&P ranked down the public debt (Moody's Aaa, S&P AA+). This triggered a worldwide stock price fall.
September 2012	QE3 was enacted. The purchase amount of FRB increased from 75 billion dollar to 85 billion dollar per month.
May 2013	The debt of the federal government reached its revised ceiling again.
October 2013	The Houses permitted to extend the fiscal ceiling with a time limit.
January 2014	FRB decided to reduce the purchase amount of public debt from 85 billion dollars to 75 billion dollars per month.
February 2014	The Houses admitted to lift the ceiling of public debt.
May 2014	FRB reduced the purchasing amount from 55 billion dollar to 45 billion dollar per month.

must note that there are scarce incidents within Japanese economy that make stock prices soar.

Because one is unable to find a persuasive reason of the stock market boom since 2013 within the domestic economy, this fact leads us to consider overseas incidents. It should be emphasized that the U.S. economy suffered the appalling fiscal crisis from 2008 to 2014.

Table 4.1 is a chronological summary. Huge fiscal deficits forced the quantitative easing monetary policy (QE policy). The utmost QE policy (QE3) recorded that FRB pledges to purchase the public debt of the United States that amounts 85 billion dollars per month (September 2012). Such QE policies were unavoidable because the federal government encountered the ceiling of the deficit twice (May 2011 and May 2013). This provoked lowering of the credit rating of the public debt issued by the U.S. government in August 2011. As such, it should be noted that it was no wonder that the evacuation from dollar assets was realized when Abe took his office.

Figure 4.6 illustrates the inflow of stock option to Japanese economy. It peaked at 2012. Stock options are purchased at about 1.9 trillion yen.

Figure 4.7 corresponds to the inflow of funds for purchasing Japanese stocks. This recorded 1.6 trillion yen at 2013 soon after the huge purchase of stock options during 2012.

This suggests that all most options were exercised and converted to Japanese stocks. One must, herewith, note that the seeds, which triggered the boom in the Japanese stock market, had been already sowed before the 2nd Abe cabinet was formed. Additionally, one must acutely note that, as illustrated in Figure 4.8,

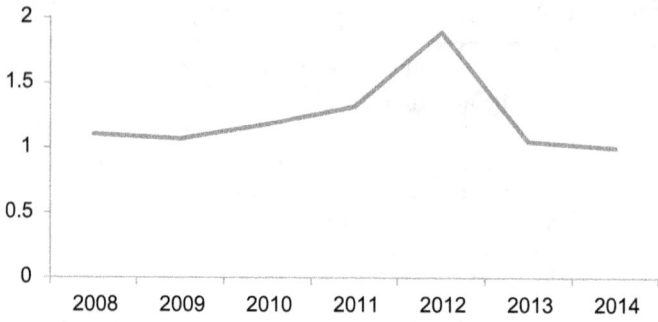

Figure 4.6 Foreigner's holding option (BOJ: trillion yen)

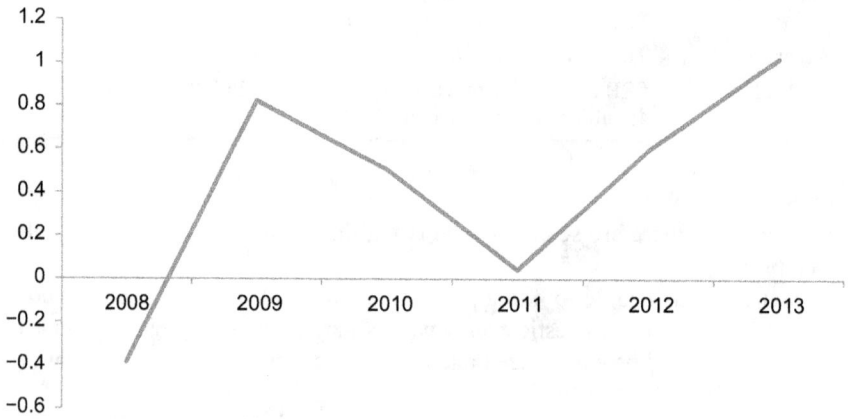

Figure 4.7 Inflow of stock purchasing (BOJ: trillion yen)

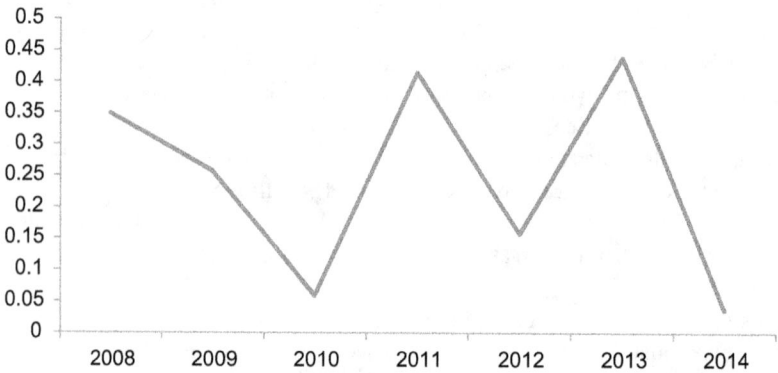

Figure 4.8 Outflow of stock from domestic financial intermediaries (BOJ: trillion yen)

Japanese financial intermediaries were sellers of stocks throughout this era. As such, there was no peculiar power for regaining the stock market boom to the domestic economy despite the spurious propaganda of Abenomics.

In this sense, the boom owes much to the instability of the U.S. economy rather than to Abenomics. It seems that the allegation that Abenomics contributes to the stock market boom is illogical and a kind of fuss. It is the very fact that the formation of the 2nd Abe cabinet coincided with the financial crisis in the United States.

4.4   The sudden depreciation of yen and Abenomics: deterioration of the balance sheet of BOJ and Its economic consequences

Based on the *fundamental equation* derived in Chapter 2, we can distinguish the foreseen steady inflation from the fierce and abrupt hyperinflation that originates from the disbelief in the value of money. As long as people are confident in the value of money, the equilibrium inflation rate obeys the solution of Equation 4.10 if the total employment L_t is kept constant. In this sense, a *sound* inflation is essentially a real phenomenon unrelated to the supply of monetary assets.

Nevertheless, one must note that the fundamental Equation 4.10 contains an indeterminate value. That is, while this equation enables to determinate the equilibrium inflation rate, the current absolute value of the price is questionable unless the assumption of the confidence to the value of money is upheld. Such indeterminacy stems from the genetic and fragile characteristic of a monetary economy. In other words, whenever the *confidence* to the value of money is impaired and people become to believe that money will become worthless sooner or later, the current value of money is immediately devalued, and prices of goods and services soar. Only in such a malignant case, inflation is a purely monetary phenomenon.

Let the initial equilibrium inflation rate be ρ. Then the equilibrium price sequence is denoted as

$$\left(p_{t-1}, p_t, p_{t+1}, \cdots\right) = \left(p_{t-1}, \rho p_{t-1}, \rho^2 p_{t-1}, \cdots\right) \tag{4.11}$$

as far as the credibility is maintained. The equilibrium value p_t in Equation 4.11 takes an unperturbed unique value subject to the fundamental equation. This means that the inflation caused by real incidents such as a change in labor productivity is predictable and mild. On the other hand, if the current prices jump up by the collapse of the confidence, then

$$\left(p_{t-1}, p_t, p_{t+1}, \cdots\right) = \left(p_{t-1}, \lambda p_{t-1}, \rho \lambda p_{t-1}, \rho^2 \lambda p_{t-1}, \cdots\right)$$
$$\lambda > \rho \tag{4.12}$$

holds. λ denotes the initial jump of the price level caused by the disbelief in the intrinsic value of money.

Equation 4.12 means that the inflation provoked by monetary incidents is quite volatile and possibly entails a devastating effect to a monetary economy incomparable with the inflation due to real incidents because λ can take any arbitrary value.

One should note that there is an upper limit of money supply permissible to a central bank. The confidence to the value of money, although it might be implicit, is collateralized by its hoarding precious metals and credible foreign and domestic assets that are ensured as worldwide transaction media and stores of value. Taking the current aversion to the additional tax levying into consideration, although it is quite precarious, public debts are liable to be monetized and are easily convertible to the debit side of BOJ's account. Hence, as the first approximation for assessing the prudence of BOJ, it might be plausible to deduct the stock of the public debt from assets of BOJ.

As Figure 4.9 indicates, BOJ's assets have been piled up about twice (26 trillion yen) during these six years.

This never means that the performance of BOJ as the central bank is excellent. On contrary.

Figure 4.10 shows the change of the BOJ's assets excluding the stock of public debt that mainly consist of BOJ's loan, foreign reserve and hoarding corporate debt. These can be regarded as sound assets owing to their confirmed solvencies.[7]

According to Figure 4.10, the stock of such assets was drastically reduced by 1.5 trillion yen (about 25 per cent compared with the maximum) since the exorbitant expansionary monetary policy accelerated in 2013.

As exhibited by Figure 4.11, the soundness of the balance sheet of BOJ has grievously deteriorated, in the sense that vast liquidity is provided (see Figures 5.3 and 5.4) without sufficient endorsement by surely solvent assets.

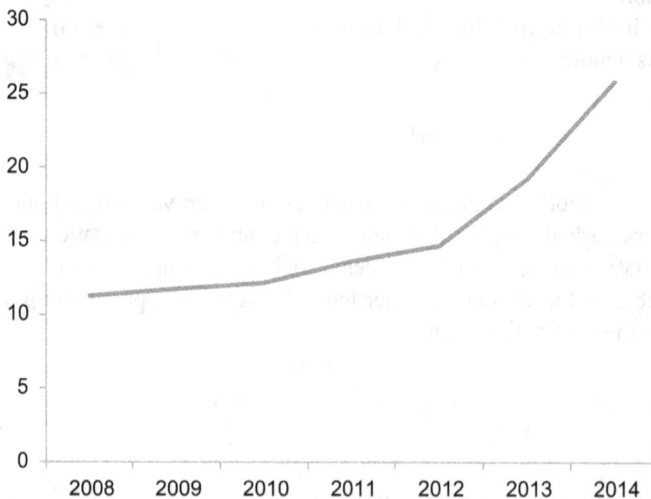

Figure 4.9 Total asset of BOJ (BOJ: trillion yen)

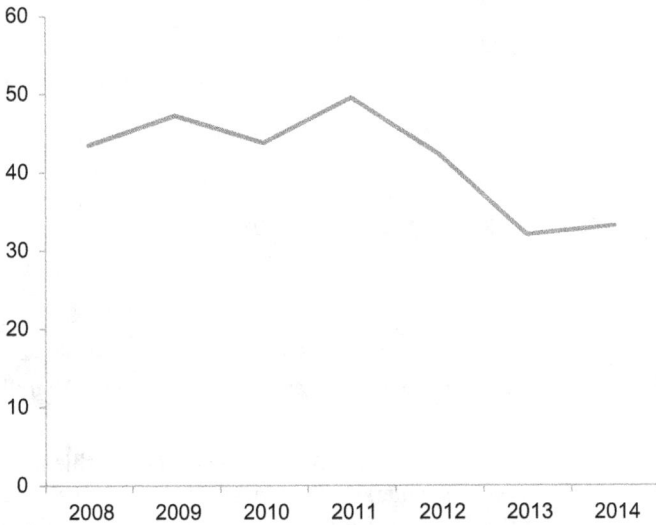

Figure 4.10 Asset of BOJ (excluding public debt) (BOJ: trillion yen)

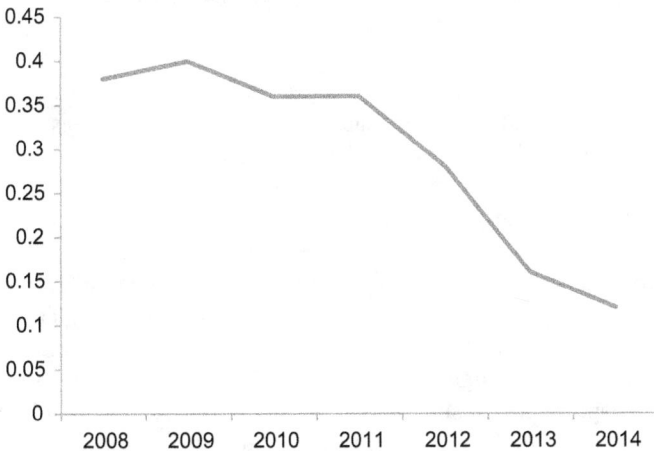

Figure 4.11 Ratio of BOJ's sound asset to total asset (BOJ: trillion yen)

This fact implies that the liquidity, which BOJ provides without impairing the *confidence* to the value of money, approaches to or possibly exceeds the upper limit. The succession of the exorbitant expansionary monetary policy is quite precarious because such policy triggers uncontrollable high inflation although the inflation may be caused somewhat indirectly as discussed below.

The causality will differ from the past experiences of hyperinflation as long as most Japanese citizens, who do not have precise knowledge about what the fiscal

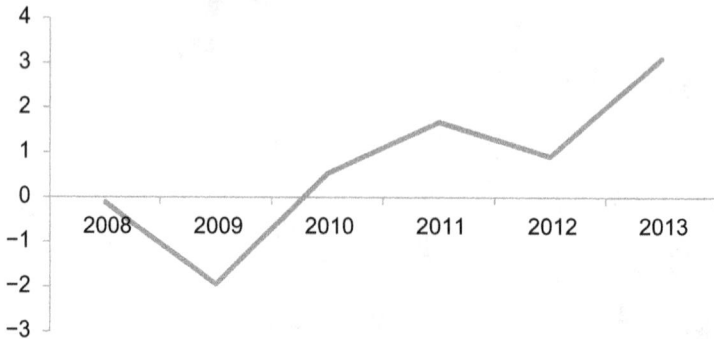

Figure 4.12 Overseas security investment of financial intermediaries (BOJ: trillion yen)

crisis means, are still confident to their currency. The uncontrollable inflation will creep from the foreign exchange market. The deterioration of the balance sheet of BOJ mainly bothers professional investors such as financial intermediaries. Along with the significant interest difference, the fear for the collapse of the confidence to yen urges them to huge foreign security investment.

Figure 4.12 illustrates the outflows of the security investment. The line is the sum of the flows of the overseas lending and security investment with reselling condition of domestic financial intermediaries.

There are two prominent appalling features. One is that overseas security investment rapidly advances after the Lehman shock despite the fiscal crisis of the United States. Specifically, this surmounts to 1.8 trillion yen during 2011. This fact suggests that there is a deeply rooted precaution to the collapse of the confidence to yen at least among Japanese financial intermediaries.

The other is that the above tendency is exacerbated by the exorbitant expansionary monetary policy. As exhibited in Figure 4.12, the new overseas security investment soared up to about 3 trillion yen during 2013. This amounts to about one-third of the excess reserve of Japanese financial intermediaries deposited in BOJ. Although BOJ attaches 0.1 per cent interest to the excess reserve, it is apparent that such a temptation does not succeed in locking the effect of the exorbitant expansionary monetary policy within the domestic economy.

Such movement surely induces the depreciation of yen. This potential pressure in the foreign exchange market did not become prominent until the fuss in the Japanese stock market due to the serious fiscal crisis in the United States unreasonably dispersed. This is because the huge purchase of yen occurred at the same time as the stock purchase by foreigners, and hence this moves the nominal exchange rate to the opposite direction. After the fuss was gone, this counterbalance power also disappeared. As such, the nominal exchange rate abruptly depreciates from about 80 yen per dollar (November 2012, BOJ) to 103 yen per dollar (December 2013, BOJ).

In contrast to the advance in the disinflation of domestic goods, such a drastic depreciation of yen makes imported goods dearer, and thus it is certain that the terms of trade, which is defined as

$$\text{Terms of Trade} \equiv \frac{p^{domestic}}{p^{import}} = \frac{p^{domestic}}{\pi p^{import*}} \tag{4.13}$$

will aggravate, where $p^{domestic}$ and p^{import} are the domestic good and the imported good price levels in terms of yen, respectively. π and $p^{import*}$ denote the nominal exchange rate and the imported price level in terms of dollar. Thus, the deterioration of the terms of trade implies that citizens in home country become able to purchase less foreign goods in terms of their currency. Moreover, as long as the asset evacuation from yen continues, the latter effect will dominate the former, and uncontrollable inflation will be provoked since BOJ, even now, cannot manipulate the nominal exchange rate under the exorbitant expansionary monetary policy.

In conjunction with the domestic asset crowding out, the asset evacuation from yen also exacerbates the wage/employment conditions in the labor market. Employees like to maintain their living standards despite the deterioration of the terms of trade. While their impoverishment is partly compensated by the disinflation of domestic goods, they still need to demand higher wages to purchase dearer imported goods. Nevertheless, since the terms of trade are deteriorated, the home goods are relatively cheaper than the foreign goods. Thus, the real wage, which the domestic employers face, would be heightened. Accordingly, if employees stick to their living standard, the unemployment rate would increase. Conversely, whenever employees devote themselves to keep their employments, they would be forced to lowering their living standards.

To summarize, against its unwise intention, Abenomics (especially the exorbitant expansionary monetary policy) do Japanese economy more harm than good.

4.5   Concluding remarks

We have analyzed the effects of Abenomics in reality faithfully to objective data. Obtained results are as follows.

First, the persistent disinflation (sometimes mild deflation) owes much to the exorbitant expansionary monetary policy. The exponential enlargement of the base money and/or the widely defined liquidity requires a higher rate of return to nominal assets. Under the regime of zero-interest policy, disinflation, which enables to raise the rate of return, is an inevitable economic consequence as such.

Disinflation makes the opportunity cost of the investment to human and physical capital dearer, and such investments are retarded. This brings about the stagnation of business and the progress of labor productivity. Accordingly, against the frivolous political intention, Abenomics advances disinflation and slowdowns economic growth.

Second, Abenomics is almost unrelated to the boom in the stock market of Japan. The boom was mainly caused by the fiscal crisis in the United States. The purchasers of the stock of Japanese companies during the boom in 2013 are for-eign investors who would be averse to the default of the public debt of the U.S. Domestic financial intermediaries were minor sellers, and hence the stock market recovery did not originate from the internal power of Japanese economy.

Finally, the exorbitant expansionary monetary policy has a devastating effect on the depreciation of the nominal exchange rate. There are two economic incidents that triggered this depreciation. One is the significant difference between the inter-est rates of dollar and yen. The other is the evacuation from domestic securities that comes from the disbelief of the value of yen. Such disbelief might be distilled by the precarious deterioration of the balance sheet of BOJ.

The terms of trade is aggravated by the inflation in imported goods due to the depreciation of the nominal exchange rate. Although such a negative effect is partly mitigated by the disinflation in domestic goods, Japanese employees demand a higher nominal wage if they wish to keep their living standard. Never-theless, this demand raises the real wages that employers face. Consequently, some of employees are forced to leave their jobs. In other words, if the employees wish to keep their jobs, they are to accept a lower standard of living.

To summarize, the rapid depreciation of the nominal exchange rate in conjunc-tion with the prominent disinflation, both of which stem from the exorbitant expan-sionary monetary policy, necessarily exacerbates employees' well-being.

Notes

1 See Otaki (2015, Ch.12) for more rigorous theoretical explanation concerning the rela-tionship between the monetary policy under the zero-interest scheme and economic growth.
2 It is enough for readers who are not interested in mathematical analysis to capture the below causality intuitively and skip the formal analysis for more detail.
3 The time preference rate is defined formally as follows. Let the reference point be $c_1 = c_2$, where c_1 and c_2 are current and future consumption levels, respectively. The time prefer-ence rate ρ is defined as the tangency of the indifference curve that passes the reference point. In other words, the time preference rate represents how an individual prefers cur-rent consumption to future consumption because those who have a high preference rate require more future consumption to compensate unit reduction of current consumption. If the lifetime utility function U is the Cobb-Douglas form and

$$U \equiv [c_1]^{1-s} [c_2]^s, 0 < s < 1$$

holds, the saving function becomesin such a case. The corresponding time preference rate ρ becomes

$$\rho \equiv \frac{1-s}{s}$$

Thus, a lower value in the marginal propensity to saving corresponds to a higher value in the time preference rate.
4 One must note that lower NDP per capita $\tilde{y}$ is equivalent to lower labor productivity.
5 Such an omission intends to eliminate the roundabout effect caused by the deprecia-tion of the nominal exchange rate to CPI. CPI, which includes these commodities and

services, increased about 1 per cent during 2013. This discrepancy can be regarded as an unfavorable effect brought about by the rapid depreciation of yen that will be discussed in Section 4.4 in more detail. Furthermore, one must note that since the rate of the consumption tax has raised by 3 per cent in Japan since April 2014, the rise of CPI during 2014 is almost spurious in the sense that does not the result from the exorbitant expansionary monetary policy.

6 The subsequent sections are based on intensive and constructive discussions with Makoto Fujishiro and Masayuki Matsuyama. They enlightened me very much, although we are unable to agree on some points of my analysis. Many thanks should be given to them.

7 This definition of the soundness of hoarding assets might be rather arbitrary because the large part of the assets of Japanese financial intermediaries comprises public debts. In this sense, this definition possibly overestimates the soundness of BOJ's balance sheet.

References

Keynes, J. M. (1936) *The General Theory of Employment, Interest and Money*. London: Macmillan.

Otaki, M. (2015) *Keynesian Economics and Price Theory: Re-orientation of a Theory of Monetary Economy*. Tokyo: Springer.

Part III

The meltdown of Japanese firms

In Part III, in contrast with Part II which deals with monetary aspects of the Japanese economy, we focus on real aspects of the economy: labor markets and capital investment behavior. That is, we analyze changes in corporate governance structure and investment behavior from the Structural Reformation era. Chapter 5 analyzes whether or not changes in governance structure make management more efficient. In Chapter 6, we consider effects of the surge of foreign direct investment that is linked closely to the movement of the exchange rate.

5 The metamorphose of Japanese firms

5.1 The establishment of the dominance of stockholder

The most prominent feature of Japanese firm was precise evaluation concerning employees' dexterity. Employers were eager to promote the dexterity until the early 1990s. Since physical capital can record more efficiency by high-quality labor force (i.e., process innovation) and such dexterous employees are also rewarded by stable employment environment (lifetime employment) and relatively even wages (seniority wages), this managerial strategy motivated both employers and employees.

However, around the turn of the century, the role of employer and the power of stockholders drastically changed. Before the bust of Bubble, an employee was a moderator for the conflict between employees and stockholders, who is rather in favor of employees.

Stockholders were outsiders of firm and excluded from crucial managerial decisions. Such type of governance structure is also empowered by the huge amounts of cross shareholding between firms (Kabushiki Mochiai). This makes unrelated stockholders to the firm be marginal substantives in corporate governance. To summarize, coordination between employers and employees functioned well under the suppression of stockholders' rights until the Structural Reformation era.

Around the mid-1990s, banks began to sell their hoarding stocks to cover capital losses triggered by the bust of Bubble (their share to total stock decreased from about 40 per cent in 1994 to 20 per cent in 2009). According to Ito (2011), such stocks were mainly bought by foreign financial companies. This is evident from the fact that the share of foreign companies in total stocks rose from about 5 per cent in 1994 to 25 per cent in 2009. In addition, note that the share hoarding of non-financial companies kept almost unchanged (around 25 per cent).

Thus, foreign investors started to cut in the managerial strategy of Japanese firms. Sheltered Japanese firms from the pressure of stock market were forced to change their corporate governance structure to assimilate the Anglo-American style. They put much importance on short-run evaluation by stock market that was a marginal existence in the economy until the previous century, and strife to maximizing their market values.

That is, in conjunction with long stagnation, which impoverished earnings of firms and forced them heavily to rely on financial incomes, the very presence of foreign investor triggers the influx of short-sighted profit maximization behavior.

Such short-sighted managerial strategy provoked serious conflicts between employees and their employer, who metamorphosed to the agent in faith to stockholders. The long-run stable employment and relatively even wages were regarded as obstacles to stockholder's interest because these conventions squeezed profits.

Rapid deregulation in firing rights of employers substantially advanced during the Structural Reformation era. Meanwhile, meritocratic wage system gradually permeated into all industries.

Although such reformations might temporally recover earnings and heighten the market value of a firm by economizing various costs, advocators do not pay sufficient attention to the consistency of managerial strategies in the short run and in the long run. Furthermore, we must note that there are possibly conflicts between the maximization of profits and social welfare.

There is no alternative deep insight concerning the long-run strategy other than what supported the Japanese High-Growth era. Thus, we need to analyze ahead what kind of resources is accumulated within Japanese firms before the bust of the Bubble. We cannot advance to the next step, which shows us how we should adapt the current economic situations, until characteristics of Japanese firms in their heydays are entirely clarified.

5.2   Efficiency within firm

How a firm is managed efficiently is a fundamental issue to analyze the transformation of Japanese firm's management. We introduce the neoclassical view on firm and Coase's (1937) theory, which negates the possibility of decomposition of a firm into each production resource and asserts that the firm is genetically a complement, which market is unable to achieve.

However, Coase's theory has a crucial drawback. Although he argues that transaction costs hinder such decomposition, the substance of transaction cost is quite ambiguous. Williamson (1985) alternatively proposes asset specificity as a source of organic combination within a firm. He, nevertheless, does not succeed in clarifying what asset specificity means. To summarize, theory of a firm is entrapped by sterile controversy on the definition for characterizing features of a firm.

After discussing such preceding research, we show that dexterity that skilled employees possess is the organic bondage of production resources. For example, any machine cannot operate without dexterity of relating skilled employees. In other words, skilled labor forces bring positive externality to the working of capital. We call such externality within a firm dexterity. Furthermore we regard internalization of such externality as an acute role of firm. It is clear that the externality makes skilled labor and capital inseparable contrary to the neoclassical economics' assumption.

5.2.1 Neoclassical firm

A firm in neoclassical economics is characterized by a linear homogenous production function. Production function is a function which describes quantitative relationship between production resources and an output. In general, an increase in a resource also increases the output. For simplicity, let us assume that production resources are limited to capital and labor and denote a production function as

$$y = F(K, L) \tag{5.1}$$

where K is the quantity of capital and L is that of labor.

Linear homogenous production function has the following property

$$\lambda y = F(\lambda K, \lambda L) \tag{5.2}$$

where λ is some positive constant. To understand the meaning of Equation 5.2, let us set $\lambda = 2$ tentatively.

The right-hand side of Equation 5.2 then implies that all production resources are doubled. The left-hand side means, in conjunction with the inputs, the output is also doubled. Economically, such property means that there is no other scarce production resource besides capital and labor because there is no bottleneck in production if the employer can increase capital and labor by the same proportion.

We can also show that all outputs y are distributed to capital and labor and that the employer can get nothing. That is,

$$y = rK + wL \tag{5.3}$$

where r is the (gross) interest rate accrued by providing capital in terms of the output. w is the real wage measured by the same unit (see Appendix B for more detail of derivation of this formula).

Equation 5.3 is a natural consequence from linear homogeneity of production function. Since there is no other production resource than capital and labor, the employer contributes nothing to production process, and hence he or she obtains no reward. In other words, a firm in neoclassical economics is a mere assembly of production resources and ultimately decomposed into production resources. Everyone can easily establish a firm only by purchasing resources from markets. In this sense, a firm is dissolved into markets in neoclassical economics. However, we must note that the owner of a neoclassical firm is the employer, while he or she can get nothing in equilibrium.

5.2.2 The Coase-Williamson's theory

The main assertion of Coase (1937) is that a firm is never dissolvable into markets and that it operates as a complement to markets. In other words, a firm is an organization, which solves economic problems that markets cannot achieve.

According to Coase, what generates a firm separated from markets is the existence of transaction costs.

Transaction costs (e.g., incurred by various contract arrangements), cause scale economy. Since these costs are independent of the level of output, the unit cost per output decreases with output.

For example, let us assume the following cost function C.

$$C \equiv x + T \tag{5.4}$$

where x and T are output level and transaction costs, respectively. Then, the average cost AC is

$$AC \equiv \frac{C}{x} = \frac{x+T}{x} = 1 + \frac{T}{x} \tag{5.5}$$

AC is illustrated in Figure 5.1. We can easily ascertain that AC is downward sloping, and thus, the average cost decreases with the production scale.

In such case, mass production becomes advantageous via economizing transaction costs, and production concentrates on few firms that cannot dissolve into markets unlike a firm in neoclassical economics.

This non-dissolvability stems from the lumpiness of transaction costs. In markets every firm can purchase any quantity of production resources that match

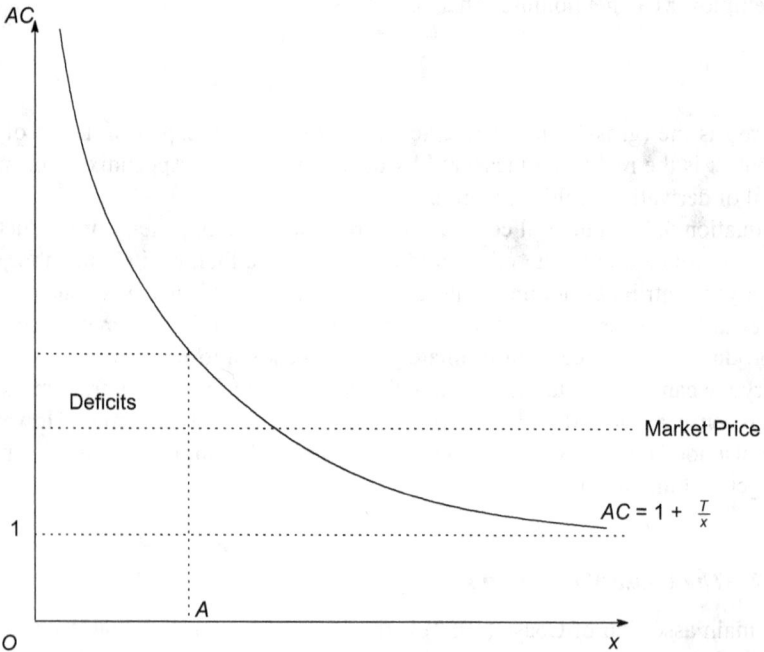

Figure 5.1 Downward sloping average cost

with its necessity. Nevertheless, the production resources that incur transaction costs are not divisible, and hence, a firm cannot choose their demand properly through price mechanism. That is, the existence of transaction costs is a cause of market failure.

If any small production is admissible as neoclassical economics assumes, there is no supply when transaction costs exist. This is exemplified by point *A* in Figure 5.1. If production limit of a firm is depicted by point *A*, the average cost is located above the market price of output *p*, and thus the firm experiences deficits. As a result, it exits from the market sooner or later. This discussion is applied to every small neoclassical firm which tries to enter the market. Consequently, a good that necessitates transaction costs for production is never provided under perfect competition where everyone can establish a firm, and free entry/exit is guaranteed.

This implies that Coase's firm, differing from neoclassical firm, is a genetic organization which functions as a complement of markets. Since, differing from neoclassical firm, a market is occupied by few oligopolistic firms that can afford to pay transaction costs, such firms have the power of price manipulation.

Figure 5.2 illustrates the monopolistic pricing. Profits are equal to zero at the intersection of demand curve *DD* and average cost curve *AC*. However, because this firm has monopolistic power, it can earn positive profit by raising the price slightly. Point B corresponds to this situation and the rectangle *BCDE* is the monopoly profits.

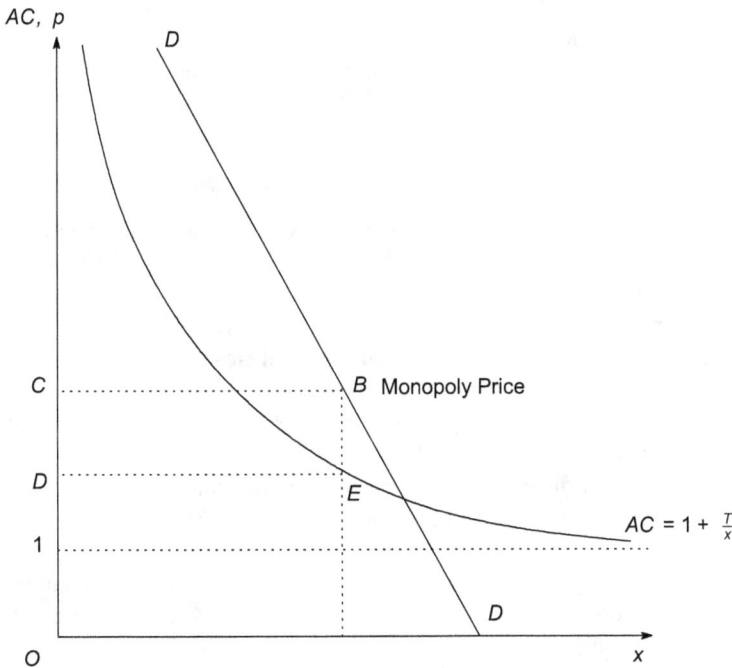

Figure 5.2 Monopolistic pricing

We must note that these profits are considered to be attributed to the employer, who is independent of the stockholders. Because the rate of return of stock is equalized to the real rate of interest, r, by interest arbitrage under certainty, there is no change in the status of a stockholder as a mere supplier of capital as in a neoclassical firm.

The monopolistic profits are rewards to unmarketable employer's labor, which is summarized the words of transaction costs. In this sense, residue claimant is not stockholders, but an employer in Coase's theory. The same discussion is applied to Williamson's (1985) specific assets. Williamson considers that some specific assets that characterize a firm and generate economies of scale are nurtured at employer's expense. Thus, differing from the tendency at present, stockholders are regarded as outsiders of a firm in Coase-Williamson's theory.

There are two serious problems in Coase-Williamson's theory of firms. One is what transaction costs and specific assets mean. The concepts proposed by them are rather vague. As discussed above, it is not difficult to prove that there is a scale economy within firm and that a firm is organized to internalize such benefit, provided that there are unmarketable production resources. However, neither Coase nor Williamson exemplifies their theoretical concept. Hence, their theories are hardly tenable to analyze actual economies.

The other reason, which makes the application of their theories difficult, is the ambiguity of relationship between an employer and stockholders. Recent research (e.g., Jensen 1986) assumes that an employer is an agent of stockholders and should maximize stockholders' benefit. That is, ultimate owner that is defined by being residue claimant is assumed to be stockholder in recent research in contrast with Coase-Williamson's theory. If an employer is the owner of a firm and transcend to stockholders, successors of Coase-Williamson should clarify the reason why such balance of power between employer and stockholder can be constructed.

5.2.3   *Uzawa-Penrose's theory: dynamic aspect of a firm*

Coase-Williamson's theory emphasizes the existence of scale economy (i.e., increasing return to scale). Nevertheless, is the growth of a firm unable to explain without such existence? Since scale economy is incompatible with perfect competition where no firm can manipulate prices and prices are determined to equalizing aggregate demand to supply, this question is related closely to the origin of a firm. That is, most firms are small in their infancy and cannot enjoy scale economy in reality. Then, how can they grow? Uzawa (1969)-Penrose's (1959) theory provides an answer to this question.

Uzawa-Penrose's theory assumes a linear homogenous production function as assumed in neoclassical firm of Section 5.2.1. As apparent from the property indicated in Equation 5.2, the size of a firm becomes indeterminate in such case. However, this theory regards capital as a quasi-fixed production resource. This is because, according to Uzawa (1969), various business skills are embodied in capital, and thus, it incurs non-negligible additional costs to accumulate capital (Penrose effect). Accordingly, a firm accumulates capital gradually but steadily, no matter how small the firm is.

Since the theory assumes that no particular skills are required for employees, and capital is the only quasi-fixed production resource, residue claimant is limited to stockholders. Current research on corporate governance and investment function is extended based on this assumption. That is, owner of a firm is stockholders and whatever harmful to their interests should be eliminated. From this view, cutting wages is one of the most favorable management strategies.

Nevertheless, it is quite an unnatural assumption that various skills necessary for sustaining and growing a firm are embodied entirely to capital. Capital actually comprises buildings, machines, computers and etc. Even though we admit that management skills are in possession of executive directors who are faithful to major stockholders and the stock price and dividends reflect to their incomes, most of skills that improve quality of output and/or efficiency of production process belong to anonymous skilled labor forces.

Once we admit the acute fact that not only stockholders but also employees invest to their firm, although there is difference in the kind of capital (i.e., physical capital or human capital), another corporate governance theory emerges.

5.2.4   Otaki-Yaginuma's theory: the model of a typical Japanese firm in the high-growth era

As is apparent from discussion in Section 5.2.3, it is natural to regard the accumulation of human capital is the acute driving force for a firm's growth. For example, machine and computer cannot achieve full capacity unless employees have sufficient skills. Moreover, process innovation and precise quality control of outputs that is the most progressive business strategy of Japanese manufacture firms become dysfunctional without incessant mutual communication between employees. This is because subtle information processing concerning such innovation demands deep mutual understanding on characteristics of each employee. Information processing necessary for coordination within a firm is an acutely delicate matter as such.

Otaki and Yaginuma (2012) and Otaki (2013) define these tangible and intangible skills as dexterity of an employee. We consider that dexterity affects positive externality to physical capital. That is, even though the stock of physical capital is kept constant, if dexterity is furnished, productivity of physical capital is improved.

Although we are in line with Coase (1937) in the sense that a firm is an existence which corrects market failure, we do not regard scale economy, which stems from the vague conception like transaction cost, as the source of such failure. Alternatively, we assert that positive externality from human capital to physical capital is the overt economic factor that a firm should internalize.

The difficulty in internalization of dexterity connects with the property right of physical capital that embodies dexterity. To clarify the discussion, let us denote explicitly the production function that we should analyze. That is,

$$y = F\big(\psi(k,L),L\big) \qquad (5.6)$$

where y is the output level. k and L are inputted physical capital and skilled labor, respectively. F and ψ are linear homogenous functions. ψ means the effective physical capital that embodies dexterity of skilled labor force.

For simplicity, we assume that physical capital is a marketable production resource and human capital (i.e., skilled labor force) is a storable resource. In addition, we set the unit price of physical capital is unity and the required rate of return is r. We denote the reservation wage (the minimal wage that incentivizes employees) of an employee as w^R.

Governance structure of a firm affects crucially its long-run growth. First, we consider the case that stockholder is residue claimant. In this case, a firm fails in internalization of dexterity, and hence, a firm under such governance structure faces ultimately the limit of growth. This is because stockholder does not evaluate the contribution of dexterity to production, and thus he or she regards it as rent accrued from owing a firm itself.

In other words, stockholders regard the production function of their firm represented by Equation 5.6 as diminishing return to scale. That is, they think that there is scale diseconomy in their firm. This perception comes from the fact that they neglect an acutely indispensable production resource: *dexterity* (See Appendix A for more detail).

Whenever a firm faces a decreasing return to scale production function, there is an optimal size of the firm. This is because costs for expanding firm increase proportionately with the firm size, while the increment of output wanes gradually in conjunction with the size. In turn, this fact implies the growth of this kind of firm converges to zero in the long run, where sufficient adjustment time elapses. Thus, the incorrect evaluation of dexterity deprives opportunities of growth of a firm.

Next, instead, let us consider the case that residue claimant is skilled employees. Stock holders merely provide physical capital, and they are outsiders of a firm. Furthermore, we assume that there are numerous unskilled employees who do not have skills to communicate with each other for developing more efficient production process and/or more high-quality goods. In this sense, unskilled employees never affect positive externality to capital, and thus, they are specialized in simple and unintelligent works.

From profit maximization conditions in the short run, we obtain

$$\left(\frac{\Delta F}{\Delta \psi}\right) \cdot \left(\frac{\Delta \psi}{\Delta k}\right) = r, \left(\frac{\Delta F}{\Delta L}\right) = w^R, \tag{5.7}$$

$\left(\frac{\Delta F}{\Delta \psi}\right)$ is the increment of output per additional effective capital, and $\left(\frac{\Delta \psi}{\Delta k}\right)$ is the increment of effective capital per additional physical capital. Hence, $\left(\frac{\Delta F}{\Delta \psi}\right) \cdot \left(\frac{\Delta \psi}{\Delta k}\right)$, which appears in the left equation of (5.7), is the increment of output per additional physical capital. This must be equalized to additional capital cost because if the former exceeds the latter, more additional profits are obtained by increasing physical capital. By the same token, the direct increment of output per additional labor $\left(\frac{\Delta F}{\Delta L}\right)$ is equalized to its additional cost w^R. This is expressed by the right equation in 5.7.

The residue delivered to skilled employees R is[1]

$$R \equiv F\big(\psi(k,L),L\big) - rk - w^R L \tag{5.8}$$

Since F is a linear homogenous function,

$$F = \left(\frac{\Delta F}{\Delta \psi}\right) \cdot \left(\frac{\Delta \psi}{\Delta k}\right) \cdot k + \left(\frac{\Delta F}{\Delta \psi}\right) \cdot \left(\frac{\Delta \psi}{\Delta L}\right) \cdot L + \left(\frac{\Delta F}{\Delta L}\right) \cdot L \tag{5.9}$$

holds (See Appendix B for more detail). Substituting Equations 5.7 and 5.9 into Equation 5.8, we obtain

$$R = \left(\frac{\Delta F}{\Delta \psi}\right) \cdot \left(\frac{\Delta \psi}{\Delta L}\right) \cdot L \tag{5.10}$$

Equation 5.10 is very important in the following two senses. First, it implies that the source of residue is the additional output originated from dexterity. That is, skilled employee improves quality of effective capital ψ, and an increase in ψ increases output F. Different from the case that residue claimants are stockholders, we must note that employees, who are substantial owners of a firm at this case, can internalize the positive externality of their skills to physical capital (i.e., dexterity). This is because skills are their own possessions.

Second, as apparent from Equation 5.10, the residue increases proportionately with skilled labor force L. This implies that there is no obstacle to the growth of a firm, differing from the case that stockholders are residue claimants. The internalization of externalities of skills is the acute cause of such constant return to scale production.

Since residues distributed per skilled employee is $\left(\frac{\Delta F}{\Delta \psi}\right) \cdot \left(\frac{\Delta \psi}{\Delta L}\right)$ from Equation 5.10, its capitalized value q is

$$q = \frac{\left(\frac{\Delta F}{\Delta \psi}\right) \cdot \left(\frac{\Delta \psi}{\Delta L}\right)}{r} \tag{5.11}$$

In contrast with Tobin's (1969) q, which corresponds to the imputed price of physical capital q represented by Equation 5.11, is the imputed price of dexterity. In this sense, q in Equation 5.11 is a human capital q. Similarly to Tobin's q theory, the accumulation of skilled labor advances whenever q in Equation 5.11 increases, and thus a firm grows faster.

To summarize this subsection, correct evaluation for dexterity is a crucial factor for firm's growth. This is because dexterity is intangible and hardly measurable asset from other's eye. It cannot be internalized without skilled employees' voluntary assessment. Hence, skilled employees as residue claimants of a firm discipline themselves, and thus promote firm's growth. This is an acute cause that supported the High-Growth era of Japan.

5.3 Economic welfare and firm's growth: the metamorphose of Japanese firm

In this subsection, we consider how governance of a firm, in which labor and capital are combined organically by the existence of dexterity, affects welfare of all constituents.

Since payments of reservation wage are cancelled out by disutility of labor, from Equations 5.7, 5.8 and (5.9), the net surplus which an employee managing firm (a firm in which residue claimants are skilled employees) earns is

$$\left(\frac{\Delta F}{\Delta \psi}\right) \cdot \left(\frac{\Delta \psi}{\Delta k}\right) \cdot k + \left(\frac{\Delta F}{\Delta \psi}\right) \cdot \left(\frac{\Delta \psi}{\Delta L}\right) \cdot L = r \cdot k + \left(\frac{\Delta F}{\Delta \psi}\right) \cdot \left(\frac{\Delta \psi}{\Delta L}\right) \cdot L \qquad (5.12)$$

The first term in Equation 5.12 is capital income which is distributed to stockholders. The second term is reward for dexterity (residue) which is skilled employee's due.

We must note that the same amount of earning distributed to stockholder even when the firm is controlled by stockholder as far as deployed capital k and skilled labor L are unchanged. Nevertheless, such assumption is not upheld. This is because an employee managing firm grows by succeeding in internalizing the externality of skills while a firm which is under the control of stockholder cannot achieve growth.[2]

It is a well-known fact that as far as prices such as r and w^R are unchanged, the ratio between deployed capital and skilled labor is also kept constant under a linear homogenous production function. Hence, the value in Equation 4.12 grows exponentially. This implies that an employee managing firm outperforms a stockholder controlling firm in the long-run. That is, precise evaluation of dexterity is an acute driving force for firm's growth.

Thus, besides an income distribution problem between stakeholders, an employee managing firm achieves higher efficiency than under the control of stockholder, who does not have much concern with employee's skills.

As discussed in Chapter 2, the decline of average productivity and economic growth rate of Japan coincides with the change of concept of justice concerning corporate governance.[3] This turn happened around the turn of century (i.e., the Structural Reformation). Before the Structural Reformation, most Japanese regard their firms as employee managing firms even though stockholders are residue claimants nominally.

In a sense, a firm had been regarded as a commons where employees share various kinds of information and refine skills to earn more residues.

However, as the Structural Reformation advances, in conjunction with the aggravation of employment environment and the erosion of cross shareholding, the decision of stockholder started to affect firm's management. Although stockholders are well-informed on firm's financial conditions, they do not possess sufficient information on organic structure of firm. As such, dexterity is underevaluated. This is a grievous economic factor that makes the Japanese economy stagnant.

5.4   Economic importance of cross shareholdings: marginalization of stock market

Harada and Hino (2002) found clearly that dividend paid out by most Japanese firms, regardless of their sizes and industries, is quite stable over time at least before the turn of century. They also found that unforeseen changes in profits are mainly absorbed by changes in retained profits, and that more than a half of retained profits are used for capital investment.[4]

These facts suggest that stockholders were not substantive residue claimants at least until the Structural Reformation advanced. It is unnatural to consider that the purpose of capital investment was reinvestment itself. In other words, it is unthinkable that most Japanese firms enjoyed their growth itself without any other purpose. Hence, fruits of a firm's growth did not necessarily appear in profits.

As Gordon (1982) points out, it is a well-known fact that nominal wages in Japan moved more flexibly than in the United Kingdom and United States. Fukao and Otaki (1993) prove that such prominent property can be explained by assuming intensive human capital investment. This is because if the investment cost is sunk, employees must be patient with stagnation to get back the cost. Thus, skilled employees, instead, became real residue claimants as discussed in Section 5.2.4.

Nevertheless, such corporate governance structure changed drastically around the turn of century. As apparent from Figure 5.3, the total dividend recorded in

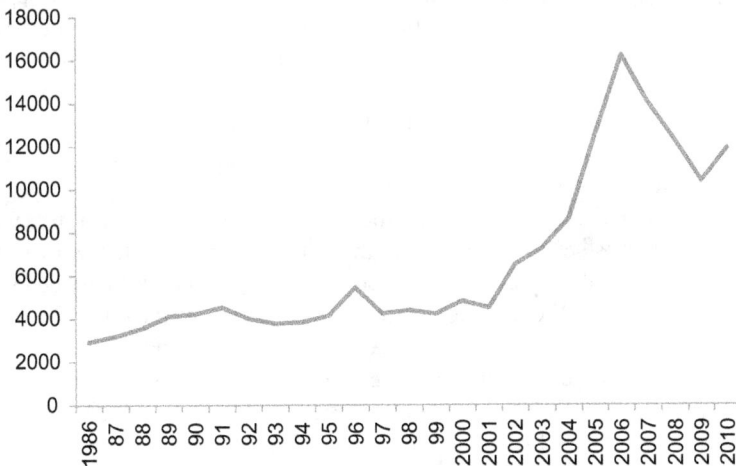

Figure 5.3 Dividend (billion yen)

Financial Statements Statistics of Corporations by Industry (Ministry of Finance) soared about by four times compared with the 1990s. Furthermore, the total dividend becomes quite sensitive to business cycle. This is also contrastive with the stable total dividend during the 1990s.

These facts imply that the presence of stockholders is empowered, and they become residue claimants instead of employees. We must note that the governance structure excluding stockholders from managerial decision, which was a dominant structure in Japanese firms, was sustained by marginalization of stock market. The acute measure for this marginalization is the wide prevalence of cross shareholdings.

For example, assume that an economy comprises two corporations, A and B. If A and B mutually hold 51 per cent of their issued stocks, the stock market is marginalized if both managers in A and B intend to establish employee managing firms. Even though 49 per cent outside stockholders want to affect financial decisions of such firms, this is surely shuttered at general meeting of stockholder. Thus, marginalization of stock market by cross shareholdings was the corner stone for maintaining employee managing firm.

As discussed in 5.1, intensive cross shareholdings were dissolved during the 2000s. Although, according to Nitta (2006), there is still acute difference between employer and stockholder concerning the direction of dividend policy,[5] it can be undeniable that corporate governance centering on stockholders interests become prevalent in conjunction with the dissolve of cross shareholdings. This is an appalling economic heritage from the bust of Bubble in early 1990s.

5.5 Conflict between managerial right and economic efficiency within firm

As we discussed in Sections 5.3 and 5.4, as far as a firm is organized and united organically by the existence of dexterity, there is an intrinsic conflict between the Anglo-American thought concerning managerial right, in which interests of stockholder are prioritized, and economic efficiency within firm as a whole. This inefficiency stems from the contradiction that those who substantially unite a firm organically are not true owners, and thus, internalization of dexterity becomes dysfunctional.

This inefficiency is illustrated in Figure 5.4.

The left small circle represents the total value added earned by a firm whose residue claimant is stockholder. Since such a firm is inefficient, the area of the circle becomes small. However, the shaded area that corresponds to dividend is far larger than the area in the right large circle, which expresses the total value added of an employee managing firm, which has the same production function.

It is clear from Figure 5.4 that although an employee managing firm is preferable socially, as far as the ownership of firm is stockholder's due, higher efficiency within firm cannot be achieved because stockholder pursuits only their own interests. Thus, wherever dexterity plays an important role, the Anglo-American type of corporate governance is not suitable from the view of social well-being.

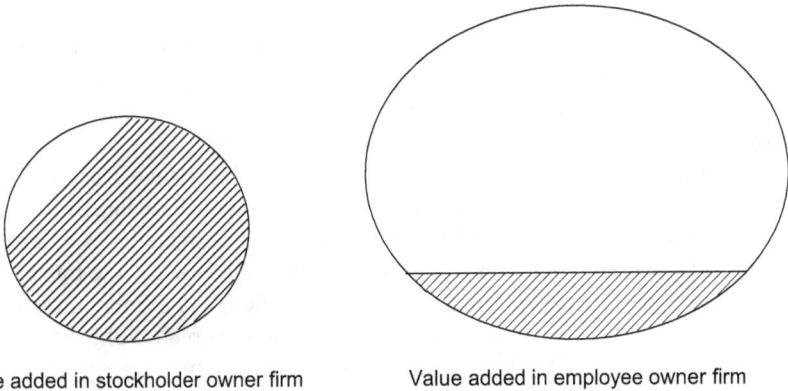

Value added in stockholder owner firm   Value added in employee owner firm

Figure 5.4 Conflict between managerial right and economic efficiency

5.6   Concluding remarks

In this chapter, we explored theories of firm in order to capture how Japanese firms are transformed by the bust of Bubble and the Structural Reformation. Obtained results are as follows.

1. We classified the theories into four classes: neoclassical firm, Coase-Williamson firm, Uzawa-Penrose firm and Otaki-Yaginuma firm. A neoclassical firm is only an assembly of various production resources and decomposable into market mechanism. Such approach cannot explain fatally why firm operates in different discipline from market mechanism. That is, although people in markets behave in spontaneous order, once they enter a firm, they must subdue to orders by their boss. The view of neoclassical firm cannot resolve the reason why orders are necessary within firm.

Coase-Williamson firm depends crucially on scale economy. Scale economy is incompatible with competitive market because small firms cannot survive market competition. Thus, firm emerges as a monopolistic entity. However, there is serious ambiguity in their theory. That is, their school does not succeed in exhibiting clearly what causes scale economy.

Uzawa-Penrose firm is characterized by the existence of quasi-fixed production resource, physical capital. They assume that various knowhow and skills are embodied in physical capital. It is natural under such assumption that the owner of a firm or residue claimant becomes stockholder, and thus, manager is in charge of a faithful agent to stockholder. Firm grows with the gradual accumulation of physical capital. This theory succeeds in justifying the existence of the Anglo-American type firm. Nevertheless, it is hardly thinkable that business skills are embodied in physical capitals (buildings, machines, computers and etc.) that are under the control of employees.

Conversely, Otaki-Yaginuma's theory assumes that skills and knowhow are embodied in employees through formal trainings and experiences (learning-by-doing). This theory implies not only that skilled labor force affects positive externality to physical capital (dexterity), but also that it needs time to nurture skills and knowhow.

In a case that skilled labor becomes quasi-fixed production factor instead of physical capital, it is natural that residue claimant are employees' due. This type of corporate governance is also socially efficient, because of the abovementioned positive externality naturally internalized.

2. By using Otaki-Yaginuma's theory, we evaluated the change in corporate governance of Japanese firm between the High-Growth and the Structural Reformation era. It is ascertained that one of the most prominent characteristics of Japanese firms during the High-Growth era is the virtuous cycle between the transcendent internalization of dexterity, which employees develop, and a firm's growth. Furthermore, we observed from various data that the governance shifted from the employee managing firm to the Anglo-American type. This was triggered by the collapse of cross shareholdings and the de facto deregulation concerning the firing rights of employers that will be discussed in more detail in Chapter 6.

3. As far as the business strategies of most Japanese firms are process innovation to create cheap and refined goods depending on employees' dexterity, such change in corporate governance brings about inefficiency by failing the positive externality to internalize. This discussion is at least partly verified by the stagnant of labor productivity as revealed in Chapter 2 and Hayashi and Prescott (2002). Consequently, metamorphose of Japanese firms from employee managing firm to the Anglo-American governance is considered to lower the efficiency of Japanese firms and injure social well-being of the Japanese economy.

Appendix A

In this Appendix, we prove that the perceived production function that neglects the existence of dexterity becomes diminishing return to scale. Let us separate the increment of output into the contribution of each production resource. From Equation 5.6, we obtain

$$\Delta y = \left(\frac{\Delta F}{\Delta \psi}\right) \cdot \left(\frac{\Delta \psi}{\Delta k}\right) \cdot \Delta k + \left(\frac{\Delta F}{\Delta \psi}\right) \cdot \left(\frac{\Delta \psi}{\Delta L}\right) \cdot \Delta L + \left(\frac{\Delta F}{\Delta L}\right) \cdot \Delta L \qquad (A.1)$$

Δx means the increment of x. $\left(\frac{\Delta F}{\Delta \psi}\right)$ is additional output acquired per additional effective physical capital. $\left(\frac{\Delta \psi}{\Delta k}\right)$ is additional effective capital acquired per additional physical capital. $\left(\frac{\Delta \psi}{\Delta L}\right)$ is additional effective capital per additional skilled labor force, which means the positive external effect of dexterity. Finally, $\left(\frac{\Delta F}{\Delta L}\right)$ is additional output acquired per additional labor force (including unskilled labor force).

From profit maximization condition, we obtain

$$\left(\frac{\Delta F}{\Delta \psi}\right) \cdot \left(\frac{\Delta \psi}{\Delta k}\right) = r, \quad \left(\frac{\Delta F}{\Delta L}\right) = w^R \qquad (A.2)$$

The above conditions imply that additional output per each production resource (the left-hand side of each equation) should be equalized to its additional cost. This is because a firm will gain more profits if additional output exceeds its cost.

Substituting Equation A.2 into A.1, we obtain

$$\Delta y = r \cdot \Delta k + \left(\frac{\Delta F}{\Delta \psi}\right) \cdot \left(\frac{\Delta \psi}{\Delta L}\right) \cdot \Delta L + w \cdot \Delta L \qquad (A.3)$$

Finally, by rearranging terms in A.3, we can ascertain that the following inequality holds:

$$\Delta y > \Delta y - \left(\frac{\Delta F}{\Delta \psi}\right) \cdot \left(\frac{\Delta \psi}{\Delta L}\right) \cdot \Delta L = r \cdot \Delta k + w \cdot \Delta L \qquad (A.4)$$

By multiplying some positive constant λ, on both sides of Equation A.4, we obtain

$$\lambda \cdot \Delta y > \lambda \cdot r \cdot \Delta k + \lambda \cdot w \cdot \Delta L \tag{A.5}$$

Equation A.5 indicates that the perceived production function of a firm, which does not evaluate the positive externality of skilled labor, $\left(\frac{\Delta F}{\Delta \psi}\right) \cdot \left(\frac{\Delta \psi}{\Delta L}\right)$, is diminishing return to scale. This is because even though all inputs are increased by λ times, the increment of output is less than λ.

Appendix B

In this appendix, we shall sketch the proof of the formula in Equation 5.9. Since F is a linear homogenous function, for any arbitrary positive number λ,

$$\lambda F = F\left(\psi(\lambda k, \lambda L), \lambda L\right) \tag{A.6}$$

holds. Applying Equation (A.1) to (A.6) (note that we fix k and L and regard F as a function of λ), we obtain

$$\Delta\lambda \cdot F = \left(\frac{\Delta F}{\Delta\psi}\right) \cdot \left(\frac{\Delta\psi}{\Delta k}\right) \cdot \Delta\lambda \cdot k + \left(\frac{\Delta F}{\Delta\psi}\right) \cdot \left(\frac{\Delta\psi}{\Delta L}\right) \cdot \Delta\lambda \cdot L + \left(\frac{\Delta F}{\Delta L}\right) \cdot \Delta\lambda \cdot L$$

$$\Leftrightarrow F = \left(\frac{\Delta F}{\Delta\psi}\right) \cdot \left(\frac{\Delta\psi}{\Delta k}\right) \cdot k + \left(\frac{\Delta F}{\Delta\psi}\right) \cdot \left(\frac{\Delta\psi}{\Delta L}\right) \cdot L + \left(\frac{\Delta F}{\Delta L}\right) \cdot L \tag{A.7}$$

This corresponds to Equation 5.9.

Notes

1 We deduct the payment for reservation wage to measure net earnings that bring positive utility.
2 Most executives in Japanese firms are, especially by twentieth century, promoted by employees. In this sense, there is hardly serious conflict between employers and employees within an employee managing firm.
3 Hayashi and Prescott (2002) estimate these declines using a more sophisticated method.
4 Astonishingly, according to Harada and Hino (2002), most of retained profits were reinvested into capital during the 1990s, which is spuriously called 'the lost decade.'
5 Nitta (2006) reports that about 70 per cent of employers wishes to keep their dividend as it was before, but that more than 70 per cent of stockholders demand that dividend should be distributed in accordance with firm's profits.

References

Coase, R. H. (1937) The nature of the firm, *Economica, 4,* 386–405.
Fukao, K. and M. Otaki (1993) Accumulation of human capital and the business cycle. *Journal of Political Economy, 101,* 73–99.

Gordon, R.J. (1982) Why U.S. wage and employment behavior differs from that in Britain and Japan. *Economic Journal, 92,* 13–44.

Hayashi, F. and E.C. Prescott (2002) The 1990s in Japan: a lost decade. *Review of Economic Dynamics, 5,* 206–235.

Harada, Y. and N. Hino (2002) Distribution between labor and capital and disposition of profits (Rodo to shihon no bunpai, rieki shobun). Financial Review (Ministry of Finance), pp. 102–123.

Ito, M. (2011) Cross shareholding: the history and perspective (Kabushiki mochiai no hensen to tenbo), *Kinyu,* pp. 16–24.

Jensen, M.C. (1986) Agency costs of free cash flow corporate finance, and takeovers, *American Economic Review, 76,* 323–329.

Nitta, K. (2006) Reconsideration on dividend policy: can dividend policy enrich stockholders? (Haito seisaku saiko: haito seisaku ha kakunushi kachi wo takemeruka?) Nissay Kisoken Report, pp. 1–8.

Otaki, M. and H. Yaginuma (2012) The growth of a firm and the accumulation of human capital: a conflict between managerial right and firm's growth (Kigyo seicho to jinteki shihon no chikuseki: keieiken to kigyo seicho no konhurikuto), DBJ Discussion Paper Series 1208, Research Institute of Capital Formation, Development Bank of Japan.

Otaki, M. (2013) The evaluation of dexterity and a theory of the growth of a firm. *Modern Economy, 4,* 226–229.

Penrose, E. (1959) *The Theory of the Growth of the Firm.* Oxford: Oxford University Press.

Tobin, J. (1969) A general equilibrium approach to monetary theory. *Journal of Money Credit and Banking, 1,* 15–29.

Uzawa, H. (1969) Time preference and the Penrose effect in a two class model of economic growth. *Journal of Political Economy, 77,* 628–652.

Williamson, O.E. (1985) *The Economic Institutions of Capitalism.* New York: Free Press.

6 The surge of foreign direct investment and the industrial hollowing

6.1 Deregulation of the labor market and FDI

The Structural Reformation has rapidly advanced foreign direct investment (FDI), mainly towards East Asian economies. As discussed below, the de facto dismissal rights of employer are remarkably strengthened, and thus FDI was implicitly subsidized during the Structural Reformation. The former was enacted by the deregulations of the Worker Dispatching Act (WDA; Rodosha Haken Ho) and the Employment Security Act (ESA; Shokugyo Antei Ho). These deregulations have drastically widened the opportunity for hiring untenured employees, specifically in the manufacturing industry. As such, dismissing tenured employees has become quite easy compared with the High-Growth era, and the bargaining power of employees concerning wage/employment negotiation is thwarted rapidly throughout the Structural Reformation era.

The deregulations of the WDA and ESA and the surge of FDI are the other sides of the same coin. For utilizing the cheap and abundant labor force in the East Asian economies, it is necessary to close many domestic factories and offices. The above deregulations facilitate employers to adopt such ruthless employment policies. Furthermore, since employees fall in weaker position, they are forced to accept the lower wage offers as such.

The resultant high unemployment and low wages aggravate business within the domestic economy because these incidents are quite harmful for the domestic aggregate consumption. This implies that there is a serious conflict between an individual firm and national interests. That is, while the cheap labor force in the East Asian economies fascinates Japanese manufacturing industry, most citizens are suffered from the surge of FDI.

In addition, the economic hollowing, which is defined by the fact that an industry moves most of its domestic production bases overseas, is a kind of *fallacy of composition*. As discussed above, the surge of FDI deprives the purchasing power of a nation as a whole. The impoverished citizens give up purchasing high-quality but expensive goods produced in Japan, and instead, switch to cheap goods provided by the East Asian firms. Thus, Japanese manufacturing industry lost their domestic markets in exchange for the overseas markets.

It is an unwise decision for the industry as a whole. The domestic markets are intrinsically most advantageous and fascinating markets because firms find no serious difficulties in arranging logistics, and moreover, they are immune from the risk of the exchange rate. Thus, the economic hollowing is a typical example of the fallacy of composition in the sense that the benefits of an individual firm do not imply those of the industry as a whole.

There is another fallacy of composition in the surge of FDI. It relates to the endogeneity of the real exchange rate. The real exchange rate is an exogenous variable for a firm that is never affected by its economic activities, and hence the firm misunderstands that the cheaper labor force in the East Asian countries is beneficial. However, whenever we remind the remittance of earnings, it is found that such an easygoing FDI policy is erroneous. No matter how multinational firms earn profits in overseas markets, if they should intend to remit the profits simultaneously, such an economic behavior appreciates the real exchange rate widely. This implies that the increment of profits in overseas markets is almost cancelled out by the appreciation and that the increased profits by the business upturn in overseas countries become almost nil in terms of the domestic currency. Accordingly, it should be noted that FDI under a flexible exchange rate system is unable to earn more profits as it looks. This is the second fallacy of composition concerning the surge of FDI.

6.2   Why are Japanese wages high compared to those in the East Asian countries?

What triggered the surge of FDI is the wage differential between Japanese and East Asian economies. Accordingly, as a preliminary step, it is necessary to analyze why such differentials emerge.

There is a well-known theorem in international economics that is dubbed the *factor price equalization*. This theorem is a kind of the application of the law that one good should possess one price. Considering that there are twin countries, whose production technology is identical: one unit labor produces one identical good. This good is tradable among international economies.

The factor price equalization theorem advocates that the real wages are equalized by trade even though labor is immobile. This can be easily shown as below. Let p^h and p^f denote the absolute price of the home and foreign country's good, respectively.[1] W^h and W^f are the nominal wages of each country. When perfect competition prevails within each country, the zero-profit condition requires

$$p^h = W^h, p^f = W^f \tag{6.1}$$

If opportunities of free trade are opened, as the result of the competition between firms,

$$p^h = p^f \tag{6.2}$$

holds. By Equations 6.1 and 6.2, we obtain

$$W^h = W^f \tag{6.3}$$

This is the simplest example of the factor price equalization theorem.

This theorem asserts that, as long as there is no substantial technological gap, the international arbitrage of the good price induces the equality of labor income. However, it is undeniable that the wages of Japanese employees are significantly higher than those of the East Asian employees. Hence, there should be economic incidents that this theorem neglects.

Above all, the existence of non-tradable goods such as housing service and infrastructure is a crucial factor for explaining the wage differentials. To illustrate this, let's assume that the labor markets both in the home country and the foreign country are competitive in the sense that every employee can switch his or her employment in response to the real wages. In addition, when trade begins, the price of tradable good, p_h^T, is kept intact.

Furthermore, suppose that the home country is initially a self-sufficient economy and that the foreign country is under development and there is no tradable industry. Then, the equilibrium nominal wages, which are equalized to the nominal reservation wages and prices, are

$$W_h = W_h^T = W_h^{NT} = p_h^T = p_h^{NT},$$
$$W_f = W_f^{NT} = p_f^{NT} \tag{6.4}$$

where the subscripts (h, f) denote the symbols of the home and the foreign country. The superscripts (T, NT) indicate the characters of the tradable and the non-tradable industry. If, due to the scarcity of land available for urbanization and/or industrialization, the domestic reservation wage, which is the minimum wage that incentivizes employees, is higher than that in the foreign country, then

$$p_h^{NT} > p_f^{NT} \Rightarrow W_h > W_f \tag{6.5}$$

holds. It is apparent from Equation (6.4) that the home country is a high-wage country. The wage differential is ensued as such. That is, the very existence of scarce immobile production resources is an acute cause of the international wage differential.

When the economies are opened and cheap, and abundant labor force in the foreign country becomes available, the wage differential brings about the devastating effect to employees who belong to the tradable industry of the home country. This is because the domestic wage stays at the level of the non-tradable industry, and consequently, the tradable industry rushes to FDI for seeking cheaper labor force. Thus, we obtain

Definition 6.1

The industrial hollowing is defined as the phenomenon when non-negligible amounts of employees lose their jobs by the surge of FDI induced by the

international nominal wage differential. In addition, such a differential is unavoidable because the scarcity of immobile production resources such as land.

6.3 A chronology of the deregulation of the Worker Dispatching Act (WDA; Rodosha Haken Ho) and the Employment Security Act (ESA; Shokugyo Anntei Ho)

However, since employment conditions in Japan had been firmly guarded by the Labor Standards Act (Rodo Kijun Ho) before the mid-1990s, most employees were tenured. Accordingly, it is necessary for advancing FDI mainly toward East Asian economies to deregulate the act by some roundabout way. This is because the substitution of untenured East Asian workers for Japanese workers requires strengthening of dismissal rights. That is, deregulations in the WDA and the ESA play crucial roles that are depicted by Table 6.1 (quoted from Yanagisawa 2008).

The deregulation advanced through two routes. One is to extend the permissible range of industries for accepting dispatched employees. The other is more provocative. Nominally, the range and qualifications of the job mediation is drastically deregulated to enhance turnover and ensure the next job. Nevertheless, such a movement grievously impairs the *fidelity* of the job-mediation industry. Especially, the abolishment of ban in 2003 that a job mediator cannot have another job is the most problematic revision. Under such a regime, a job mediator is unable to be immune from his benefits from another business. We cannot ever exclude the precariousness that a job mediator unfairly informs his customers of excessively favorable working conditions about his related business. In conjunction with the enlarged business chances in the job mediation as it was described above, such precariousness becomes more serious. This can be regarded as an acute background of frivolous advertisements that urges the advantage of changing occupation. It should be emphatically noted that, even in a market economy, some regulations

Table 6.1 The deregulations of the Worker Dispatching Act and the Employment Security Act

1. 1996: A Revision of the Labor Dispatching Act: the extension of the admissible age of employment of dispatched employee.

2. 1999a: A Revision of the Labor Dispatching Act: Labor dispatching becomes de facto free except for the manufacturing industry. The contract term with a dispatched employee is limited to one year.

3. 1999b: A Revision of the Employment Security Law: Job mediation becomes de facto free. The mediation fee is also deregulated.

4. 2003a: A Revision of the Worker Dispatching Act: The contract term of a dispatched employee is extended from one to three years. The dispatching to manufacturing industry is permitted.

5. 2003b: A Revision of the Employment Security Law: The ban that a job mediator has another job is entirely abolished.

Quoted from Yanagisawa (2008).

are indispensable because of the imperfectness of information, monopoly power, and etc. In other words, a market economy, which lacks the necessary regulations for its sound working, is a kind of the *despotic capitalism* that is defined in Chapter 1. This is because such self-guarding regulations are firewalls to overcome the conflict of interests that mainly comes from the imperfectness of information.

The deregulation of the Worker Dispatching Act enlarges the share of untenured employees to the total number of employees. According to Labor Force Survey by Ministry of Internal Affairs and Communications, about 90 per cent of employees was tenured in 2004, and that share devastatingly fell to about 60 per cent in 2014.[2] In conjunction with the frivolous advertisement by job mediation companies discussed in Chapters 1 and 2, the turnover rate soars especially in the younger generations. As the statistics indicates, most jobs offered are untenured. Thus, by deregulations such as this one, the Worker Dispatching Act and the Employment Security Act become almost ineffective in reality.

Since the prevalence of untenured employees strengthens the dismissal right of employers, this facilitates to close domestic factories and offices to advance FDI. Such a grievous trend also weakens the wage bargaining power of employees, and this is one of serious causes of the current income disparity in Japan as depicted by Tables 6.2 and Figure 6.1.

Table 6.2 The long-run change in the income distribution

Data/Period	1986–1990	1991–2000	2002–2009
Era	Bubble Era	Lost Decade Era	Structural Reformation Era
National Income (trillion yen)	30	37	36.2
Employer's Total Income (trillion yen)	6.7	7.2	8.8
Employee's Total Income (trillion yen)	19.9	26.6	26.1

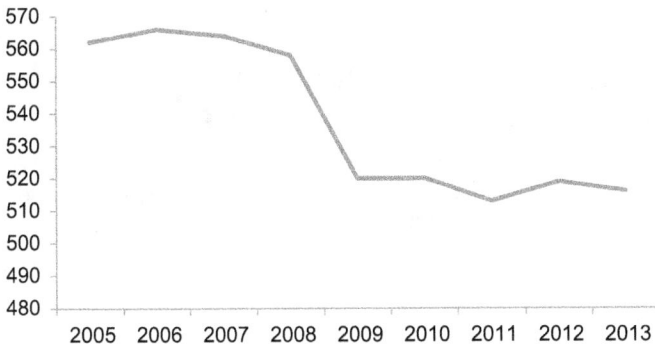

Figure 6.1 The nominal wage

Table 6.2 shows macroeconomic data based on SNA statistics (Cabinet Office) concerning the income distribution between employees and employers. Table 6.2 elucidates the aggravation of income disparity from the Structural Reformation Era. Despite the fact that the employers income increased by 1.6 trillion yen, 0.5 trillion yen of the employee's income was reduced.

Figure 6.1 illustrates the time profile of the nominal wage per annum of a worker (male; high-school graduated; 42.5 years old) calculated from the data in the Basic Survey of Wage Structure (Ministry of Health, Labor and Welfare). The wage decreased by approximately 10 per cent compared with the highest in that decade. Since there is substantively no change in the Consumer Price Index as discussed in Chapter 2, one may find with no difficulty that standard citizens in Japan face hardships in their daily life even though they are tenured.

In addition, as discussed Chapter 5, if a firm comprises organic entities based on the close communication between employees (i.e., coordination behavior), the shortsighted employment policy by an employer paralyzes the genuine function. This inevitably aggravates the labor productivity as analyzed in detail in Section 6.5. Table 6.1 provides important information. Although worker dispatching became almost free by 1999, manufacturing industry, which is still a main industry in the sense that Japan heavily depends on its export capacity, had been excluded from the list until 2003. This very fact implies that men of common sense in Japan fear that the shortsighted employment policy is hazardous for nurturing intrinsic skills embodied in employees.

The difference of the accumulation of necessary skills can be partly reflected in the difference of the nominal wages. According to the Basic Survey on Wage Structure (Ministry of Health, Labor and Welfare), the averaged nominal wage of untenured employees is about only 0.6 times of that of tenured worker. Furthermore, it should be also noted that even for tenured employees, the average nominal wage per annum (male; 40 years old) is about 5 million yen (see Figure 6.1) that decreased by 1 million yen compared with the wage before the Lehman Shock. One can easily imagine that many Japanese are impoverished by the deregulations of the Worker Dispatching Act the Employment Security Act as scape goats in the surge of FDI that seeks lower wages mainly in East Asia economies.

6.4   Macroeconomic analysis of industrial hollowing under a flexible exchange rate system

It might frighten naïve neoclassical economists, who believe in the relevancy of Heckscher-Ohlin-Samuelson theory (HOS theory), that we emphasize appalling results brought by the surge of FDI. However, HOS theory is upheld only within a barter economy in which there is no idle production resource such as unemployment. As shown in Chapter 2, in a dynamic monetary economy, the price level per se is not determined so as to equilibrate the demand and supply, but is determined by the confidence in the future value of itself. Thus, income/employment adjustment is unavoidable to equilibrate the good market.

In other words, HOS theory asserts that a capital-abundant and labor-scarce country, not in the absolute sense but in the relative sense, can improve its economic welfare by exporting capital and importing labor. This is because the domestic capital exported can earn much rent overseas, and imported cheap labor produces cheap goods. Although the income distribution might become more unequal, some redistribution policy can dismiss such a misgiving.

Nevertheless, it must be noted that HOS theory does not pay much attention to the conditions of demand. This owes to the Say's law that penetrates the naïve neoclassical school. The labor intensive industry absolutely expands and the capital intensive industry shrinks by such an international factor movement (Rybcszynski Theorem) as far as their relative price is kept constant. If the country is negligibly small relatively to the world market, this assumption is verified. Thus, any would-be idling resources are absorbed by this inter-industrial adjustment.

Since free trade is assumed, such a country does not find any obstacle against importing good, which is in shortage on the domestic market, in exchange for its surplus at a given international relative price. Accordingly, no essential problem concerning the lack of aggregate demand exists.

Nonetheless, HOS theory presumes that all individuals consume their incomes at one time. It is quite an unrealistic assumption. In reality, working individuals save some substantive part of their incomes in the form of money preparing for their retirement.[3] Meanwhile retired individuals enjoy the consumption from saved money. Thus, money is transacted by generation to generation. To summarize, the following relationship holds:

Income = Working Individuals' Consumption
+ Retired Individuals Consumption. (6.1)

While retired individuals' consumption is limited by the real money supply deflated by the price level,[4] the total income decreases whenever working individuals' income is reduced and so is their consumption.

FDI surely deprives of the income the domestic working individuals through an increase in unemployment. Although one may argue that the effect of availing cheap labor force in developing economies is also favorable to the home economy, this effect is merely an income transfer from the domestic employees to the employers, and hence there is no stimulus to the economy.

For example, assume that 10,000 home-country employees are replaced by the same number of the employees in a developing country. Further assume that the wage differential is 1 million yen per annum. Then, the cost-saving effect for the firm amounts to

$$1(million) \times 10(thousand) = 10(billion) \text{ yen}$$

However, if employees in the tradable sector had accepted 1 million yen in wage cuts, which is not unrealistic assumption when we observe Figure 6.1, the cost-saving effect would be the other side of the same amount of the wage reduction.

Hence, while the cost-saving effect possibly aggravates the income disparity between employees and employers, this does not contribute to the expansion of effective demand. Thus the effective demand remains intact because this effect is merely the income transfer from domestic employees in the tradable industry to their employers.[5]

Rather than the cost-saving effect, an increase in the number of unemployed individuals adjacent to FDI whose income is significantly lower than the income of employed is appalling. This decreases the aggregate consumption of the working individuals inevitably. Consequently, the surge of FDI lowers the domestic consumption and income, and results in the stagnation of the home country. That is, it is not too exaggerated to recognize that the acute vice of FDI stems from its importing unemployment.

In addition, the leakage from the additional income increases along with the advance in FDI because wage payments from the tradable industry to foreign employees became non-negligible. This implies that the value of the fiscal multiplier is lowered and the effect of the aggregate-demand management policy is curtailed. Consequently, the surge of FDI makes it difficult to stabilize the domestic economy.

To summarize, the effects of FDI to a home economy via the labor market have two aspects. One is the implicit income transfer from the domestic employees to their employers by the usage of cheap labor force in developing economies. Insomuch as the marginal propensity to consume is identical between them, this hardly affects the business of the home economy. The other is the serious deprivation of employment opportunities for citizens in the home economy. This is caused by the substitution of the domestic labor for the cheap overseas labor. Since, differing from the above-mentioned income transfer by cutting wages, earned labor incomes are entirely out-flowed from the domestic market, the domestic aggregate consumption grievously decreases, and so does effective demand. Thus, the depressive effect provoked by the initial increment of unemployment is amplified by the multiplier process.

The remaining question is whether earned profits overseas can offset the above detrimental effects in the home country. In conjunction with FDI, overseas markets tend to be extended. If such an extension in business enriches the FDI firm enough, FDI possibly enhances the economic welfare of a home country.

However, it belongs to a kind of the fallacy of composition. One must note that while the exchange rate is an exogenous variable for an individual firm, this variable is endogenously determined in the home economy as a whole. For example, when new and large overseas markets in East Asian economies are ensued by Japanese FDI and the export from the related factories increases, the FDI firms purchase some substantial amount of yen and sell the corresponding dollar to remit earnings to Japan. Consequently, yen appreciates. This implies that earned profits in terms of dollar are almost vanished by the appreciation of yen, or at the least, that value in yen is grievously deteriorated. That is, FDI does not pay so much as it looks because it provokes the appreciation of a home currency caused by the surge of remittance to the home country.

In other words, an isolated FDI in the sense that other firms will still stay within the home country is beneficial as far as the wage differentials exist as analyzed in Section 6.2 because the exchange rate remains unchanged. Nevertheless, if many

FDI decisions are made at one time, earnings adjacent to these decisions are large enough to affect the exchange rate because the remittable foreign exchange is extravagant. Clearly, it is a kind of the fallacy of composition. To sum up, one must distinguish the macroeconomic consequence which comes from a single economic agent from that is caused by the surge of many economic agents.

Furthermore, this process is cumulative. The triggered appreciation of the exchange rate by a surge of FDI widens the wage differential between developed and developing economies more seriously. Many firms of developed economies find additional opportunities for cost saving, and thus this ushers further FDI in. Ideally, this cumulative process continues until no firm that produces tradable goods exists within the developed economy (perfect industrial hollowing). In such a case, the leakage of overseas wage payments in the tradable industry is the utmost, and as a result, the surge of FDI or the industrial hollowing stagnates and devastates the economy.

Thus, substantial profits are not earned by FDI in terms of a domestic currency except for the key currency country. Accordingly, the most appalling economic consequence is an increase in the number of unemployed individuals that adjoin the contraction of effective demand.[6]

6.5 Difficulties in the transmission of employee's skills: the negative effect of FDI in the long run

6.5.1 General skills have been nurtured within a firm

In Chapter 2, we assert that the impoverishment owing to mass unemployment impairs the stability of daily lives of citizens, and income disparity becomes serious. As a result, educational opportunities in school and family for non-wealthy families are heavily hampered. It can be regarded as one of serious causes of the productivity stagnation and dysfunction of a firm as an entity as depicted in Chapter 5. These grievous economic conditions hinder the development of the fundamental intelligence that is indispensable for deep understandings on human nature and its society.

The exorbitant monetary expansion by Abenomics also narrows educational opportunities within a firm. Almost all young employees are not only uneducated as a constituent of a firm, but they also lack the common sense that is necessary for nationals in Japan. These appalling phenomena are partly due to the substantially high opportunity cost for human resource development brought about by the exorbitant expansionary monetary policy as clarified in Chapter 4. That is, the exponentially expanded nominal assets require a higher return to equilibrate the market. For this purpose, under the zero-interest policy, disinflation or even deflation is an unavoidable consequence. In this sense, the real interest rate is heightened by the exorbitant monetary policy, and this remarkably retards the investment into human capital.

As mentioned above, the surge of FDI is one of the causes of mass unemployment.[7] Moreover, this is an acute catalyzer of the prevalence of untenured work.

In conjunction with the exorbitant expansionary monetary policy of Abenomics, the surge of FDI seriously aggravates the quality of labor in Japan. This is because the intensive investment to human capital, which was the most prominent characteristics of Japanese firms at least by the 1970s, is hindered, and despised by employees themselves.

Such appalling phenomena clearly indicate that Japanese citizens cannot structurally comprehend how their various and excellent skills have been nurtured and are being astray in this globalization era. Some superficial economists and teachers of business schools insist that most employees' skills, in heydays of Japan, were firm specific, and never applicable to another firm, and the formation of such skills was supported by the long-term employment system (Shushin Koyo Sei). General skills, which can be deployed to more broad fields and suitable for the globalization, cannot be nurtured by the specific and narrow-ranged education within a firm.

However, we should pose this light-headed thinking, and instead, invoke the very fact that a firm-specific skills-based Japanese firm develops many original and excellent goods, and by these, the firm once overwhelmed the world market, where language, culture, religion, and so on are quite different. If skills are purely firm specific and narrow scoped, how is this high performance achieved? It is natural to consider that general skills, which are imperative factors for overseas trading, were nurtured within a firm or an industry.

Against the intuition of lay people, who do not have much concern with moral philosophy, most general skills closely relate to deep interests and inquiries about human natures that are beyond culture, tribe, language, religion, and so on. Virtues of sincerity, diligence, and integrity are the acute common universal and fundamental languages that are indispensable not merely for business, but also for maintaining a long-run partnership. The very contents of general skills are these virtues.

They are not necessarily related to MBA or PhD. These degrees are neither organic nor directly applicable by themselves to unformatted problems that ordinary employees face at their daily jobs. In reality, once a problem is clearly formatted, almost all problems become solvable and move to technical domain. Scholastic and exiting knowledge acquired in graduate school cannot be effective until a problem is clearly formatted.

The most difficult problem within an organization is to find the source of the problem and how to format it to be solvable. Such elaborating process requires the devotional cooperation between the constituents of the section or the organization as a whole. Without the virtues mentioned above, employees are not firmly tied and disbelieve one another. This triggers the curtailment of labor productivity. The personal evaluation before the prevalence of the dominance of stockholder is mainly based on the development of these unmarketable virtues of employees from the *long-run view*. This is symbolized as the following fact. That is, most presidents of Japanese firms were selected from excellent employees.

Thus, general skills for sound firm's growth are nurtured within a firm. In other words, the incumbent thesis that asserts that firm-specific skills are inferior to general skills and that the former are alienated from the latter is improper and far from reality. Although it cannot be denied that there were some feudal and oppressing aspects in Japanese firms before the Structural Reformation Era, one also cannot neglect the reverent fact that a firm is a kind of commons where employees acquire socialized thinking through formal and informal education within a firm. In this sense, a Japanese firm was a substantial substitution for schools and developed general skills through various experiences and the intellectual interpretation of them. That is, firm-specific skills generated general skills.

6.5.2   Education as incessant human growth

In conjunction with unintelligent macroeconomic policies by Abe cabinet, the surge of FDI and the harsh wage sagging ensue the deregulations of the WDA and the ESA. In the short run, such policies might earn higher profits by the reduction of production and selling costs. Nevertheless, it is clear that the growth of labor productivity is stunted in Japanese firms. This is the very evidence that unmarketable human assets were accumulated within a firm and the deregulations along with FDI erode these intangible but indispensable assets as discussed in Chapter 5.

In current Japanese firms, only marketable (decomposable to an individual) and tangible human assets are put much importance on. As discussed in the previous subsection, these assets run when a problem to be solved is clarified and formatted explicitly. Furthermore, most problems in reality are somewhat ambiguous at the beginning, and even after it is formatted, the exact formulae, which employees are taught at their university and/or graduate school, are scarcely applicable to the problem. Some skillful transformations and estimates are required for completing the job.

However, many young Japanese, who are regarded as intellectuals, are apt to react conversely. If a difficulty, which they face, is not solvable by their accumulated abilities, they would defy the reality ipso fact, and realign it at their discretion so as to apply their thin-layer knowledge. How arbitrary that is!

For developing the pragmatic skills, in which the fundamental formal education at school is permeated, education from the long-run viewpoint by superiors and intensive and sincere discussions, by which young employees are mutually enlightened, are urgently required. In addition, through the experience of elaborating education, those who are superior in ability are also educated. This is partly because such new experience develops their own skills, partly because it nurtures the depth of their abilities for understanding the human relationship. As Dewy (1916) argues, education is an incessant growth as a human being.

Those good customs were not scarce within the numerous excellent companies in Japan unrelated to their scales (one might even find that small manufacturing companies are the very core of Japanese economy). However, the short-sighted deregulations in conjunction with FDI devastatingly deteriorated such cohesion within a firm. Employees are isolated from one another because evaluations on their performance are short-sighted, and based on the concept that the contribution of each employee to the firm is divisible. As such, the development of the pragmatic skills, which needs intensive and deep communication, has almost vanished from Japanese firms. This is regarded as one of the acute causes of the stagnation of labor productivity and grievously sagging nominal wages.

6.6   Concluding remarks

In this section, we discuss the macroeconomic effects of the surge of foreign direct investment (FDI) to Japanese economy in relation to the deregulation of the domestic labor market. These are the results:

1. The surge of FDI mainly towards East Asian economies originates from the nominal wage differential. Because of the urbanization, industrialization and narrowness of the suitable residence area, the price of land is incomparably high in Japan. The expensiveness of non-tradable goods, which are almost shielded from international competition, owes much to such high land price. It is natural that higher nominal wages are demanded to keep some reasonable living standard. This is the reason why nominal wages in Japan are so high in comparison to East Asian economies. The deregulations of the Worker Dispatching Act (WDA) and the Employment Security Act (ESA) enable mobilization of the employment mainly in the manufacturing industry from Japan to East Asian economies. This triggers the surge of FDI. Consequently, the unemployment rate in Japan gradually increases, and nominal wages are sagging, especially after the Lehman Shock.

2. The cost-saving effect of FDI, which is born from employing cheap labor force in East Asian economies and/or sagging wages in Japan, is depressive to the home economy because FDI surely deprives of the domestic purchasing power. In this sense, the surge of FDI belongs to the fallacy of composition. Even though FDI develops new profitable markets, by the prominent appreciation of the nominal exchange rate, remittable capital incomes in terms of yen are thwarted. A vicious cycle emerges: the pressure of remittance of FDI's earnings appreciates yen, and such appreciation advances FDI further because the nominal wages in East Asian economies in terms of yen decrease. Again, the pressure of the remittance becomes high, and thus the nominal exchange rate further appreciates, and so on.

3. The above conclusion is a short-term appalling effect of FDI. The final conclusion is concerned with the effects in the long-term. Naïve economists consider that the liquidation or mobilization of labor market is welfare improving because unreasonable entry/exit obstacles are removed and free competition prevails. However, one must note that free competition can contribute to well-being only when the quality of labor is identical and information concerning the behavior of employees is perfect. Nevertheless, there is a significant vintage effect in employees' skills. As discussed in Chapter 5, an organization including a firm is an autonomous order to solve problems that the market cannot find any effective solution for. The nurtured skills within a Japanese firm, which are ultimately connected with the pragmatic general skills in the long run, are a typical asset that market cannot provide because a stable and non-anonymous employment environment, which excludes shameful opportunism, is necessary. Such an ingenious order is devastatingly impaired by the deregulations of WDA and ESA. One can argue that the retard of labor productivity progress reflects this appalling fact.

Notes

1 For simplicity, it is assumed that both countries use the same money, and thus the nominal exchange rate is fixed to unity.
2 It should be noted that there is no category of dispatched employee in the statistics of 2004. Accordingly, it cannot be denied that we overestimate the ratio of tenured employees in 2004. However, it should be also emphasized that there was no debris of the word corresponding to the *dispatched employee* even in daily life by the turn of the century in Japan.
3 See Otaki (2011, 2015) for a more precise and rigorous explanation.
4 It should be noted that a monetary economy is a nested structure as discussed in Chapter 2. Hence, by the fundamental equation of monetary economy, the current price level is insensitive to a change in conditions that determine the level of effective demand.
5 We here assume that the tradable goods market is under monopolistic competition where a firm faces a downward-sloping demand curve that contains the level of effective demand as a parameter. In addition, we neglect the auxiliary expansionary effect of an increase in the real cash balance approximately.
6 There are two diagnoses against the appreciation of a home currency. One is that an affiliated company in a developing economy does not remit its profits but retains them in terms of the key currency. The other is the emigration to the developing country, by which a firm can get rid of the remittance problem. Nevertheless, the former is a myopic postponement of the problem. The latter is far more serious, once one recognizes how light-hearted emigration policies provoked numerous conflicts between emigrants and their host countries. At least, personally, the author can never accept such a historically precarious policy.
7 Recently, the unemployment rate in Japan sagged under 4 per cent. However, one must note that most of the increased employment opportunities belong to untenured works. It is precarious to compare the unemployment rate in Japan with the rates older than a decade without taking the change in employee's status into consideration.

References

Dewy, J. (1916) *Democracy and Education*. London: Macmillan.
Otaki, M. (2011) *Essences of Heisei Depression: From the View Point of Employment and Finance* (in Japanese) (Heisei Fukyo no Honshitsu: Koyo to Kin-yuu kara Kangaeru). Tokyo: Iwanami Shoten.
Otaki, M. (2015) *Keynesian Economics and Price Theory: Re-orientation of a Theory of Monetary Economy*. Tokyo: Springer.
Yanagisawa, F. (2008) Deregulations of the labor laws during these ten years (in Japanese) (Saikin 10 Nen ni okeru Rodo Ho no Kiseikanwa). Reference of National Diet Library. http://www.ndl.go.jp/jp/diet/publication/refer/200804_687/068705.pdf#search='%E6%B4%BE%E9%81%A3%E5%8A%B4%E5%83%8D%E6%B3%95%E3%81%AE%E8%A6%8F%E5%88%B6%E7%B7%A9%E5%92%8C'

Part IV

Towards the reincarnation of Japanese economy

In previous chapters, we have critically examined the structure of current Japanese economy. Based on these critiques, this part considers how we reconstruct the economy and regain the cohesive society with vigor.

7   We still have time and power

7.1   A comparison of macroeconomic performance with Germany

The preceding chapters critically and structurally analyzed current Japanese economy. Do those discussions suggest that Japan has no time for resilience and will fall into a more devastating situation? The answer to this question, which I provide, is negative. Since Japan still has one of the excellent advanced economies, although we should not be excessively optimistic, there is enough time to regain the innate vigor of Japanese insomuch as incessant and patient efforts are poured as discussed below.

To wipe out the pessimism, which is prevalent in Japan, let us reconfirm the position of Japanese economy in the world.

Most economists might have the following impression. That is, Germany has achieved the Industry 4.0 (so-called the fourth industrial revolution) and become the strongest nation in EU. In contrast with German economy, Japan was troubled by the non-performing debt problem for a long time. Innovation is stagnated, and the economic prospect has been thwarted. Is this a proper investigation of both economies? Although it is a limited observation that requires a deeper and more precise analysis, let's examine the macroeconomic performances of both economies.

Table 7.1 reveals that it is not easy to judge which economy is superior. Gross domestic product (GDP) per capita, an index which represents the average physical abundance, is almost the same in both countries. The unemployment is significantly lower in Japan although it has risen by 3 per cent compared with the High Growth Era. Accordingly, Japanese economy still records good performance no less than German economy at the present stage.

However, the low inflation rate is low in both countries, it is lower in Japan. Judging from these low rates, money is confident in the sense that residents of both nations believe the intrinsic value of money and the price levels are independent of the nominal money supply. In such a case, the inflation rate is determined by two factors as studied in Chapters 2 and 4.

One is labor productivity that affects the inflation rate from the side of the real economy. Whenever labor productivity stagnates, since an employee earns less

Table 7.1 The macroeconomic statistics of Japan and Germany
IMF World Economic Outlook (five years averaged between 2010 and 2014)[1]

Country	Japan	Germany
GDP per capita (hundred dollars)	430	430
Inflation Rate (CPI)	0.5	1.7
Unemployment Rate	4.3	5.8
Public Debt per GDP	203	80
Surplus of Current Account per GDP	1.9	6.2

[1] The inflation rate in Japan reflects the effect of the increase in consumption tax rate in 2014.

nominal wage, he or she cannot tolerate the current inflation. Hence, firms cut their prices in conjunction with wage cutting. Thus, the degeneration of labor productivity provokes disinflation. This is another interpretation of the theory described in Chapter 2.

The other factor is the real balance of nominal assets that comes from the monetary aspect of the economy. Whenever the supply of nominal assets, including money and the public debt, increases, a higher rate of return is required for equilibrating asset markets as far as people are confident in their intrinsic value. Since the rate of return for nominal assets under zero-interest policy is equal to the inverse of the inflation rate, the huge accumulation of nominal assets also brings about disinflation. This is the concept of the *asset crowding out*, as labelled in Chapter 4.[1]

To summarize, the lower inflation rate suggests the stagnation of labor productivity and/or the excess accumulation of nominal assets. From such a view, the low inflation rate and/or disinflation are unfavorable phenomena. In this sense, Japan might hold deeper and more serious problem in the long run.

The public-debt stock ratio to GDP is far worse in Japan. However, one must note that about 90 per cent of the public debt is held by Japanese. In this sense, the fiscal hardship, which Japan faces, is genetically a domestic problem. Compared with the international huge non-performing debt problem (i.e., Euro Crisis), which Germany faces, the Japanese debt problem seems more tractable in the sense that it is far from the conflicts between sovereign powers. In addition, taking the instability of Euro into consideration, the high export ratio to GDP does not necessarily indicate the good performance of German economy. This is because the surplus in the current account implies the progress of lending to foreign countries and further accumulation of the foreign assets.

Thus, at present, the macroeconomic performance of Japan vis-à-vis Germany is not as different as it is asserted. However, both countries are bothered by the impaired sovereign's balance sheet.

As such, there is no economy that does not face the appalling problem due to globalization. That is, there is no unique success model to mimic in the world, and policy measures are articulated in accordance to the political economic situations where each economy is located. If one may regard Germany as the most advanced and soundest economy, Japan also have sufficient time to oust the despotic capitalism and reconstruct a harmonious society before the fiscal collapse is realized and the income disparity is incurable. Fanatic nationalism and lightheaded radicalism can solve no problem. As Burke (2009) advocates, only steady gradualism can lead us to the cohesive society.

In what follows, I shall propose and discuss some important subjects for regaining our vigorous and democratic society.

7.2   The evacuation from the myopic policy decisions

Most Japanese fiscal and monetary policies are based on quite shortsighted and imprudent prospects. Generally, the impudent behaviors of relating politicians and bureaucrats stem from the irresponsibility. It is not their concern what follows after they leave their charge, and the utmost concern is how to upturn the business temporarily no matter how devastating economic consequences are resulted in thereafter. Meanwhile, the next section shows that biased and lightheaded information provided by mass media is the most serious origin of promoting such a frivolous political atmosphere.

As examples below, let's consider the cases of the exorbitant expansionary monetary policy and the reckless plans for the 2nd Tokyo Olympic in 2020 and the Linear Motor Car project.

7.2.1   The exorbitant expansionary monetary policy

The mitigation of the exorbitant expansionary monetary policy is urgent in current Japanese economy. Despite the initial intention, this policy evidently fails to recover business and to overcome disinflation and/or deflation. As discussed in Chapter 4, since the glut of nominal assets requires a higher rate of return of them for equilibrating the market, under the zero-interest policy, it is clear that disinflation or deflation advances to guarantee such an additional rate of return. This retards economic growth and the progress of labor productivity through heightening the opportunity cost for the physical and human capital investment.

In other words, fanatic advocates of the exorbitant expansionary monetary policy are only naïve captives of the quantity theory of money that has been apparently rebutted by the recent experience both in Japan and the United States. In this sense, those who have common sense can hardly deny that the exorbitant expansionary policy fails in recovering the economy.

However, the adjoining negative effect is quite serious. The risk of the price volatility of the public debt is exceedingly concentrated into BOJ. As depicted in Chapter 4, BOJ purchase the public debt that at least amounts to 6 trillion yen from 2013 to 2014. Since the interest rate of the short-term pubic debt is around 0.1 per cent, the market price of a 6 trillion yen public debt is around

$$60000 \div [1 + 0.001] \approx 59900 \, (billion)$$

By a change in BOJ's monetary policy or by the market force, when the short-term interest rises up to 1 per cent, which is still far lower than the Treasury Bills rate in the United States, the price becomes

$$60000 \div [1 + 0.01] \approx 59400 \, (billion)$$

Thus, BOJ suffers the loss of 500 billion yen by such a slight movement of the short-run asset markets, even though limiting to the newly purchasing public debt. This amount soars to about two-thirds of BOJ's profits (2014). As such, the exorbitant monetary policy is sustained by bureaucrats and politicians from myopic and irresponsible prospects.

It is clear that this policy is unsustainable. As discussed in Chapter 4, the exorbitant expansionary monetary policy exacerbates the value of yen. The nominal exchange rate has depreciated by about 40 yen per dollar from the highest value. If the policy as such continues, it is certain that the depreciation is accelerated. Because most manufacturing industries from Japan move to the East Asian economies, the rapid appreciation only aggravates the business of the import industries and their affiliates. This grim consequence is never acceptable for most Japanese.

Moreover, insomuch as the exorbitant expansionary monetary policy continues, the risk from the price volatility of the public debt is acutely accumulated within BOJ. This makes matters more difficult to raise the interest rate. A vicious cycle, which owes much to imprudent and irresponsible attitudes of BOJ, emerges: the exorbitant expansionary advances the exposure to the volatile price-risk; the more aggressive monetary policy is required to sustain the high security price. Consequently, it is evident that the exorbitant expansionary monetary policy is not sustainable.[2]

As such, it is necessary to dismiss the monetary policy from this artificial price-maintaining measure for the public debt. Once the price-maintaining policy collapses, BOJ's balance sheet is devastatingly deteriorated. This is because the evaluation of most public debt, which BOJ hoards, turns from high-quality asset to non-performing one. This might trigger hyperinflation due to extinction of the confidence in the value of currency.

To avoid such a catastrophic consequence, as the recovering process of QE (Quantitative Easing) policy in the United States suggests, the dismissal should be performed step-by-step. BOJ should gradually decrease its purchasing volume of the public debt. Then the adjacent security price sagging becomes mitigated although this sagging is unavoidable. However, one must note that this adjustment process is not bottomless. If the interest rate of Japanese short-term public debt will sit at around that of the U.S. Treasury Bills, the artificial security price-maintaining policy, which is the other side of the exorbitant expansionary monetary policy, becomes substantively ineffectual, and Japanese economy is emancipated from the fear for the collapse of the financial system as a whole.

What one should acutely note is that, under free capital mobility like today, a small country's interest rates are never able to be free from the large country such as the United States, and any policy that is against this stringent principle shall bring a devastating consequence to the nation.

7.2.2 The construction of the linear motor car: the prominent moral hazard problem

In advance of the discussion, one must note that Japan is a drastically population-decreasing country. According to the estimation of the National Institute of Population and Social Security Research, the population decreased from about 130 million (2010) to 90 million (2050). It is evident that many infrastructures such as railways, roads, and so on should be urgently contracted and reorganized efficiently. This is mainly due to the fiscal hardship that Japan has already encountered. Since the aging process advances in conjunction with the population decrease, and this implies that the number of tax payers reduces more rapidly, it is evident that one foresees that the fiscal hardship will become incomparably serious in the near future.

The Linear Motor Car is the single-railed super express, much faster than the Super Express (Shin-kansen), so that JR Tokai plans to connect between Tokyo and temporally Nagoya. The greatest part of this railway is planned to pass through underground. The president of JR Tokai, which has already been privatized, exaggerates that no one can criticize the plan because the company compensates the construction costs, which amounts to about 8,000 billion yen, by its own fund, and thus this does not impose any excess burden to citizens.

However, such an assertion is acutely shortsighted if one confers the fiscal hardship and the rapid population decrease that Japan will be obliged to face sooner or later. One must also note that there are many incumbent alternative transportation measures between Tokyo and Osaka (Tokaido Metropolitan Belt): the Tokaido Super Express; the First and the Second Tomei Highways; highly frequent fetched air lines. Most Japanese scarcely hear that the transport ability in the Tokaido Metropolitan Belt has reached its limits. They neither know the precise structure of the business model, which JR Tokai is based on about the Linear Motor Car, nor whether such a plan is viable taking into account existing transportation measures under the drastically decreasing population.

The allegation of the president of JR Tokai that the plan of the Linear Motor Car bothers no other economic agents is precarious in the sense that that company cannot ever be resilient once the plan fails and JR Tokai falls in a serious financial distress. This is because the huge amount of money will be poured into the project, and huge amount of the running costs are incurred.

As such, the reckless Linear Motor Car project might owe much to a kind of moral hazard under limited liability and shortsighted irresponsible management policy.

That is, it is a plausible conjecture that the most executives of JR Tokai implicitly expect that the benevolent rescue from the government whenever the project fails under the conventional principle is *too big to fail*. As studied in Chapter 1, such precarious and despiteful principle deepens the trough of business triggered by the bust of Bubbles in the 1990s. Moreover, judging from the current fiscal hardship of the Japanese government, the moral hazard, which might be planted within the executives in JR Tokai (one should note that main Japanese railways were formerly stated-owned), provokes a grievous future huge accumulation of the public debt.

Such a morally hazardous behavior is exacerbated by the shortsighted and irresponsible management. That is, since the completion of the Linear Motor Car is far late compared with the term that the president is in charge, he is immune from the results of the investment. Indeed, the magnificent plan is the honor to the president in charge, and it reminds of a pharaoh who decided to build his pyramid. Nevertheless, it is not his concern that citizens will be annoyed by the tax levied when the project fails because such an appalling result is revealed far after his retirement. Thus, the shortsighted and irresponsible management is incentivized.

In addition, even though the project of the Linear Motor Car is viable, the Japanese government never considers the adjoining effects. It is evident that the Linear Motor Car deprives non-negligible passengers of the incumbent Super Express (the Shin-kansen) and/or the airlines if the project succeeds. Furthermore, as mentioned above, Japan will surely experience a rapid and drastic decrease in population, and hence it is apparent that the demand for the traffic within the Tokaido Metropolitan Belt will shrink. This implies that if the Linear Motor Car attracts substantial passengers, other transportation companies (including JR Tokai itself) will be thwarted. How do we do when the domestic airlines are fatally wounded by the success of the Linear Motor Car project? Accordingly, it is evident that not only JR Tokai, but also the Japanese government become shortsighted, and that they are irresponsible to the future burden of fiscal deficit and/or the redemption of the huge public debt. There is no impartiality on the fundamental structure about the transportation system as such.

7.3   Penetrating the transparency of the information that mass media provide

The previous subsections reveal that neither executives nor politicians in Japan have the responsibilities to the subsequent generations. They are only captives of the despiteful vanity and vested interests. As Keynes (1930) suggests, the true patriotism is deeply rooted in the benevolence to the subsequent generations of his or her nation. Thomas More's *Utopia* (1516) warned that if the constituents of a community become unable to feel the benevolence from the community as a whole, such a community inevitably faces the crisis of collapse. The bondage between generations is a vital point of a nation. This is because children learn the benevolence of the society from the love and devotion of their parents although this feeling might be nurtured via somewhat roundabout way when they are young.

If parents are impoverished and the children grow under the unstable and unsound circumstances, or contrarily, if parents indulge in their vacant pleasure and do not pay much attention to the future burdens of the children (note that the huge accumulation of the public debt predicts the heavy tax levy in the future), which will provoke a huge, devastating and uneven income redistribution, it is inevitable that children will lose the loyalty to his or her nation.

One must note that the conflict between a nation and the industries is becoming prominent especially in developed countries. The typical example is the surge of FDI discussed in Chapter 6. The essence of FDI is to seek cheap overseas labor force without considering the fact that it leads to the severe unemployment problem in the home country. In addition, as argued above, the shortsighted macroeconomic policy and the managerial strategy of private big companies do not consider the well-being of the next generation sufficiently in exchange for the ephemeral prosperity of the present generation.

One of the appalling causes of such social vices is the preposterous information that the Japanese mass media provide. They concentrate to bother employees about whether they obtain or retain their jobs, and this acutely weakens the bargaining power on the nominal wage that is also discussed in Chapters 1 and 6. Indeed, the mass media even emphasize that the anxiety concerning the employment opportunities is the employees' problem because they do not possess sufficient 'skills' to fulfill the requirements of firms.

However, we have already known that sagging wage stems from the surge of FDI. That is, the mass media and the job mediators are jointly eager to attribute the aggravating employment environment to the low skillfulness of employees. It is apparent that manipulated information as such is against the truth and even immoral. The mass media and the job mediators hide the appalling background truth that is disadvantageous to employers, although we cannot distinguish whether such vicious behavior stems from their own intentions or their incompetence. They allege that employees can find many other potential good employment opportunities if they nurture the 'skills.' One must note that such 'skills' are trifle ones, such as being familiar with PC software. Thus, Japanese labor market is almost rigged by the collusion between the mass media, employers and job mediators. Thus, astray by the fragmental and inconsistent information, most employees are unable to know the true macroeconomic situations of Japanese economy.

The rigged labor market as such is apparently harmful for most citizens in Japan. While Japanese mass media emphasize that the economy as a whole will aggravate if profits of corporations decrease, one must note, as discussed above, that the divergence of interests between the national economy and multinational corporations is prominent. The rigged Japanese labor market is a typical example. In this respect, there is an acute responsibility of the mass media to provide the precise and unbiased information for sustaining Japanese economy in the future.

This problem does not stay within the rigged labor market. This extends to the intergenerational income disparity. Myopic fiscal stimulations such as Tokyo Olympics in 2020 and expansions in infrastructures discussed above accelerate the accumulation of the fiscal deficits. The exorbitant stock of the public debt provokes the intergenerational income disparity by the following way.

To capture the problem clearly, one must reflect the reason why the public debt circulates. This acutely depends on the confidence that the additional tax for the redemption of the public debt is levied from the other agents who do not hold the public debt. If the additional tax is entirely levied from the public-debt owners themselves, it is apparent that the public debt will never possesses a positive value.

However, as mentioned before, the present stock of the Japanese public debt is some 130 trillion yen. This corresponds that a Japanese owes money about 10 billion yen since current population of Japan is about 130 million. Furthermore, the hoarding of the public debt is widespread, although it might be indirect hoarding via financial intermediaries. These facts imply that almost all Japanese are substantively both deep creditors and heavy debtors.

Accordingly, the additional fiscal expansions are precarious because the current stock of the public debt reaches the critical level whether the confidence in the public debt can be preserved or not. We must note that the bailout of the public debt is a kind of levying a heavy tax, and this inevitably disperses the confidence. This is because the bailout is the imposition of the tax to its holders themselves.

If such a devastating situation is brought about, the adjacent generations to the reckless fiscal expansion era will be fatally impoverished since they lose most part of its wealth. Thus, the current rapid expansion under the Abe cabinet possibly triggers the serious income disparity between the present and the future generation.

The mass media often warned about the fiscal hardship in Japanese economy before Abe took office. Nevertheless, the fire has been entirely extinguished because precarious macroeconomic policies including the rigged labor market of Abenomics are convenient for their vested interests. They must, however, know that such a momentary attitude does not necessarily guarantee the prosperity of their children.

7.4   Growth is not imperative

7.4.1   The ineffective Growth-Enhancing Strategy that exacerbates the income disparity

As discussed in Chapter 6 and Subsection 7.3, the deregulations in the Japanese labor market aggravate the employment environments and make the bargaining power vulnerable. As a result, the nominal wages of tenured and untenured employees decreased approximately 10 per cent during this decade. Such a ferocious wage cutting is closely connected with the Growth-Enhancing Strategy (GES; Seichou Senryaku) by the Abe cabinet.

Figure 7.1 illustrates the mechanism of the GES. Curve MPL represent the marginal product of labor that implies how many additional goods are produced by an additional labor force. The intersection E_A with the horizontal line $W_A W_A$ is the point where the profit of firm is maximized. This is because the additional revenue (the marginal product of labor) is equalized to the additional cost (the wage) at this employment level.

The wage reduction ($W_A \Rightarrow W_B$), which was triggered by the cutthroat competition between domestic and overseas employees, reduces the additional cost for production. Then, employers can hire less productive employees ($N_A \Rightarrow N_B$), and increase the production ($y_A \Rightarrow y_B$) and earn more profits. Consequently, GDP grows with exacerbating the income disparity.

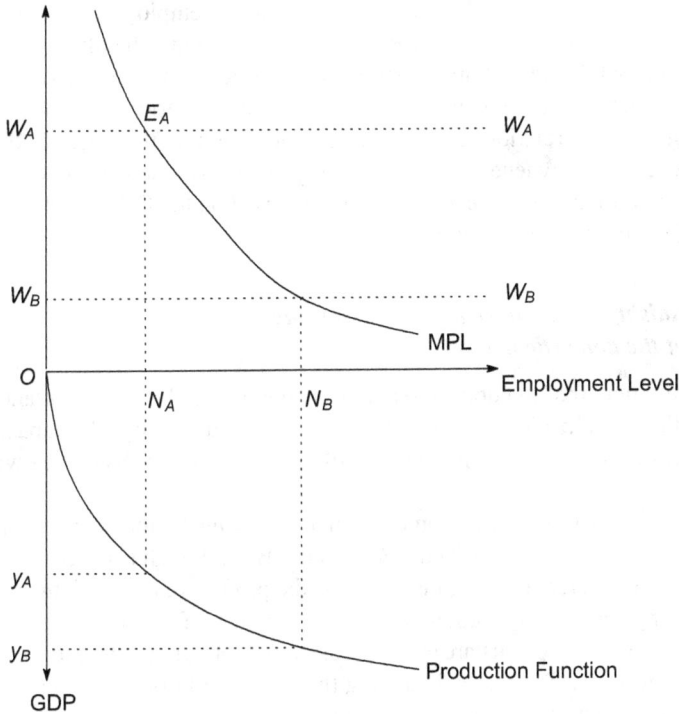

Figure 7.1 The mechanism of the GES

However, despite the ruthless wage cutting, it is apparent from Figure 7.1 that the GES has never been effective in reality. If one accepts the unrealistic assumption discussed below, it is undeniable that the total employment will be increased by GES. Nevertheless, one must note the following fact. That is, the utmost unemployment rate in Japan (2012; about 5 per cent) was recorded at the peak of FDI. This implies that most increased employment opportunities were not provided within the domestic labor market and are fled into East Asian economies that are the destinations of most FDI.

Moreover, the neoclassical-school-like GES presumes that an employer can always sell those products which he or she has produced at his discretion. In other words, GES assume the Say's law that asserts that supply creates demand. However, as a man having common sense would anticipate, this proposition is false. Whenever we admit the fact that some portion of income is saved, it is evident that, ceteris paribus, what will be saved remains to be unsold somewhere in an economy. In addition, if the receipt of the total wage decreases, it is natural to consider that the demand for goods also decreases because the purchasing power of the economy is lowered. This is because the employee's marginal propensity to consume (MPC: the additional increment of consumption brought about by the unit increase in income) is estimated to be higher than that of employers.

Accordingly, unless Japanese economy possesses affluent purchasing power, the increased outputs are only piled up in factories. If employers foresight such a grim situation, they will not increase their production, and will only enjoy lowered wages. Thus, while the GES in the Abe cabinet has no substantial positive effect on economic growth, it merely exacerbates the income disparity between employers and employees. In relation to this, one must acutely note that 'the trickle down' would never appear whenever the economic growth was based on the wage cutting by definition. In this sense, economic growth based on the GES is not an imperative subject for current Japanese economy.

7.4.2   *Raising nominal wages: the importance of the domestic market*

One should note that the domestic market is the best and most important market even in the globalization era, especially for an island country like Japan. As the advantages of the domestic market, the following factors are listed below:

(1) There is no risk in the domestic market owing to the fluctuation of the exchange rate as emphasized in Chapter 6. Even though firms earn enormous profits in foreign markets, insomuch as the profits are remitted, the adjoining exchange rate appreciation devalues the value of the remittance heavily. Otherwise, such profits are entirely consumed foreign goods (future imports), and never contribute to heightening the demand of domestic goods. That is, compared with the domestic demand, overseas earnings are not powerful as a weapon for stimulating an economy.

(2) The same language is used and customers are bred under the same culture as the firms. This facilitates the response to various and delicate needs of customers via the intensive communication. Such a process contributes to the accumulation of tangible and intangible assets and precise know-hows on the structure of the market and customer's preference. That is, the domestic market is the most efficient laboratory for developing new excellent goods.

(3) Not only the physical transportation costs but also the opportunity costs (the time necessary for gathering) are not expensive for both customers and a firm. Relatively small transportation costs create the breathing space for medium- and small-size firms from imported competing goods. The latter discussion is closely connected with point (2), in the sense that both points are concerned with the importance of communication. For developing an excellent good, it is urgently necessary to discuss intensively and analyze the vivid but fragmental information provided by customers and related firms. Face-to-face and concentrated information processing is indispensable to developing marketing know-hows because it is not easy to transmit nuances that partly, but seriously, govern the atmosphere and the efficiency of the information processing. Accordingly, the cheap opportunity costs for gathering is a fascinating factor of the domestic market.

As discussed in Chapters 5 and 6, most Japanese companies, especially those in the manufacturing industry, are lured by the low wages in East Asian economy, and forget the dominance of the domestic market, as discussed above in this chapter.

Since much of the cost (i.e., high wages) is incurred by achieving the dominance of the domestic market, the wage decreased by the surge of FDI paralyzed the following virtuous cycle that existed in the High Growth Era by the 1970s. That is,

$$\text{High Wage} \Rightarrow \text{Purchasing Power for High Quality Goods}$$
$$\Rightarrow \text{Induced Innovation} \Rightarrow \text{High Wage} \Rightarrow \cdots \cdots$$

What one should note is that the utmost marginal propensity to consume is that of the residents of the home economy, and hence they are the best customers of a firm.

It is evident from this discussion that the managerial strategy of most Japanese firm is astray from the Structural Reformation Era, where the cost reduction is regarded as the driving force of economic prosperity. Such a thought is ignorant about the fact that the purchasing power (effective demand) of an economy is the very existence that determines the prosperity. Even though a firm produces excellent goods, so far as individuals do not own a sufficient purchasing power, the consequences will not be fruitful. A simultaneous and large wage cutting belongs to *a fallacy of composition* because it is apparent that such a wage cutting lowers the purchasing power of residents in the home economy and aggravates the business against the initial intention.

Accordingly, it is urgent that Japanese firms change their managerial policies. Most of them are eager to simplify the production process so that even unskilled individuals can complete their jobs. This is a kind of *standardization* of jobs. No additional endeavor, which forms the basis of vital skills, is unnecessary, and they can be satisfied insomuch as they accept low wages. As such, the futile atmosphere, which hinders innovation, is filled within most Japanese firms. The strategy should be changed steady by using the large domestic market. To regain the virtuous above, as a preliminary step, we must raise the wages that are lost during this decade. This will make the breathing space for many employees and might promote the motivation emancipating from the *standardization* of jobs

As indicated by Table 6.2, Japanese employee lost the aggregate income of about 5,000 billion yen. Using the multiplier approach, let us calculate how much GDP is newly created by the same raise in wage, although it is a round estimation.[3] The crucial point is that there is significant difference in the marginal propensity to consume between the residents in the home country and overseas. Whenever the income legitimately transferred from overseas residents to those in the home country, the demand for the home country goods will increase without increasing the fiscal deficit.

In conjunction with the progress of the globalization, the share of overseas stock holders soared to about 30 per cent of Japanese firms (Hanazaki 2014). This fact implies that some non-negligible part of the wage hike is financed from them and that the capital income of overseas stock holders is implicitly transferred to the domestic employees through the wage negotiation. Although it is arguable that the stockholders might dislike such an implicit transfer and this brings a vicious effect to the stock market, a firm can purchase its own stocks at some low price by their affluent retained profits and hoards them. This hinders the leakage of profits to overseas investors, and an additional expansion of the demand for the home country's goods can be expected.

Excluding this roundabout effect, we can calculate the impact of a wage hike to effective demand as the following procedure. First, let's assume that the nominal wage is totally raised by 1,000 billion yen. Second, for simplicity, the marginal propensity to consume for the resident of Japan is identical and takes the value 0.7, the value which is based on National Survey of Family Income and Expenditure (Ministry of Internal Affairs and Communications). Third, the distribution rate between profits and wages is 0.25 to 0.75. Those values are calculated from Table 6.2. Finally, overseas investors are assumed not to consume Japanese goods.

Then, the sum of the ultimate fund of the expansion of GDP is sought for the capital income of overseas investors. This is because 70 per cent of the wage increment is only the transfer within Japan. Since the marginal propensity to consume is identical, such an income transfer from the domestic investors to employees brings no substantial effect to the domestic economy. Accordingly, the transfer amounts to

$$1000 \times 0.3 = 300 \text{ (billion yen)}.$$

Since the marginal propensity to consume is assumed to be 0.7, the initial increment of the domestic consumption is

$$300 \times 0.7 = 210 \text{ (billion yen)}.$$

This 210 billion yen becomes the fund of the next expansion. A quarter of the 210 billion yen will be distributed to the capital income. This amounts to

$$210 \times 0.25 = 52.5 \text{ (billion yen)}.$$

From this 52.5 billion yen, 30 per cent leaks to overseas investors. This value becomes

$$52.5 \times 0.3 = 15.75 \text{ (billion yen)}.$$

Thus, the increment of the domestic consumption in the second round is

$$210 \times 0.7 - 210 \times 0.7 \times 0.25 \times 0.3 = 147 - 15.75 \approx 210 \times 0.65 = 136.5 \text{ (billion yen)}.$$

Consequently, the total increment of the domestic consumption approximately becomes

$$210 \times \left[1 + \left[0.7 \times \left[1 - 0.3 \times 0.25\right]\right] + \left(0.65\right)^2 + \left(0.65\right)^3 + \cdots\right] = 600 \text{ (billion yen)}.$$

This figure indicates that the burden of stockholders (including overseas) for financing a 1,000 billion wage increase is ultimately about 400 billion yen (1000 – 600). Therefore, 2000 billion yen (400 × 5) is necessary for regaining the lost 5000 billion yen in wages during this decade. According to Financial Statements Statistics of Corporation by Industry (Ministry of Finance), the retained profits (excluding the financial intermediaries) during 2013 fiscal year soars about 2.3 trillion yen (the total stock of the retained profits is around 30 trillion yen). Judging from these figures, funding the 0.2 trillion yen for the wage raising is not an unreasonable demand.

If such a huge retained profits are ready for the future physical capital investment, this acutely exacerbates the uneven distribution between human and physical capital. As discussed in Chapter 5, the appalling distribution as such becomes the disincentive to employees for nurturing their skills, and deprives their breathing space at the worst. It is the gradual establishment of the despotic capitalism as defined in Chapter 1. The prevalence of the dominance of stockholder, which is directly connected with the imperativeness of economic growth, gravely impairs the self-confidence of employees and hinders the sound progress of democracy through the standardization of jobs. This is because democracy is deeply rooted in the mutual respect for the diversity of individuals.

7.5   Regaining the job diversity: farewell to expansionism

It can hardly be predicted what kind of new industry will become the key industry in accordance with an unforeseeable change in the world economy. If one defines the *expansionism* as the concentration of national resources into the present highly profitable industries to occupy the overseas markets, one must also note that the strategy as such is quite vulnerable.

This is partly because all advanced economies might pursue the strategy alike, and cutthroat competitions by the ruthless cost/wage reduction impoverish employees and affiliated small companies. In this sense, expansionism is a *pseudo laissez-faire policy* that is the measure for advancing the despotic capitalism as defined in Chapter 1.

This is partly because, as it was mentioned above, there might be an unforeseen change in the political economic structure of the world economy. The expansionism advances the specialization of an economy's industrial structure. This makes the structure of an economy stiff. Accordingly, many residents will lose their jobs once a change, which is disadvantageous to the economy's vital industries, is provoked.

If an economy ceases to pursue the expansionism, there is another story. The evacuation from the international cutthroat competition makes room for increasing wage payments and provides the breathing space for various jobs in the small and/or non-tradable sectors. The resilience of an economy is recovered as such. Even though the economy encounters an economic difficulty (e.g., a worldwide recession), the direct damage becomes far smaller than the present situation since a buffer for the tradable industry, which should now turn to find their main activities in the domestic markets, is regained.

Meanwhile, one should note that most famous Japanese firms started as very small businesses. This fact implies that the *job diversity* creates embryos of new industries, some of which will become key industries of the economy. Thus, inheriting the sufficient room for surviving small businesses is the gift for the prosperity of our descendants.

Finally, nevertheless, the confrontations with the ruthless international competition (or globalization of economies) are problematic. As analyzed in the previous section, such a competition exacerbates the income disparity within an economy to survive the competition. However, as discussed in Chapter 6 and this chapter, the globalization of economies impoverishes the *aggregate* income of a FDI country such as Japan. Consequently, the demand for tradable goods of impoverished residents shifts from the expensive goods with high quality provided by the domestic firms to the cheap ones with non-high quality by some overseas firms. Thus, there emerges the following vicious cycle that is contrary to the virtuous cycle analyzed in Section 7.4.2. That is,

Wage Reduction ⇒ Shifting to Cheap Overseas Goods
⇒ Wage Reduction ⇒ ……

This cycle warns that if the tradable-good industries continue the spiral wage reduction to survive the international competition, they will ultimately lose the domestic markets. In other words, the industries can keep their domestic markets insomuch as the wage stays within a range where employees can afford to purchase their high-quality goods, and they keep the dominance in quality by incessant innovations.

To summarize, to regain the *job diversification* under modest income equality is the acute solution for ousting the despotic capitalism in Japan. The most serious problem is that many executives in Japanese firms are entrapped by a kind of *fallacy of composition* in the following sense:

> Their best customers are their employees. If the employees are impoverished by the wage reduction, they will inevitably lose such customers, and the prosperity leaves Japan in the long run.

7.6 Concluding remarks

This chapter briefly surveys the macroeconomic performance of Japanese economy in comparison with Germany, and ascertains that Japan still has sufficient power and time for regaining the vigor. For achieving this aim, the rational gradualism is acutely required with excluding the fanatic nationalism and the old fashioned left wing.

Since subjects to be resolved are entangled, the procedure for regaining the vigorous and democratic society should be gradual. A tentative procedure is as follows:

1. Elimination of shortsighted and imprudent public policies. One must realize that the excessive public debt accumulation problem and the decreasing population problem with serious aging exist in the background of

macroeconomic policies of Japan. The stimulations to the economy, which only involve the maintenance of the current spurious prosperity, are immoral, because such policies and projects gravely disturb the income distribution of the future generations via the debt-management policy. The imprudence in the fiscal policy and the huge scale project of the private sector stems not only from moral hazard in the limited liability but also from the illusion based on the rootless *expansionism* that is a negative inheritance of the High Growth Era. It is apparent that a country with an annual population decrease of 1 per cent is unable to achieve a significantly positive growth rate in GDP. Accordingly, all the policies and projects that rely on the expansion of the economy are precarious.

2.   Penetration of the transparency and unbiasedness of the information that mass media provide. Many Japanese are in turbulence because they do not have unbiased and precise information enough to realize what macroeconomic situation they are facing as above discussed. Accordingly, the transparency of the information, which mass media provide, is required. Nevertheless, the opposite is true in reality. The labor market is rigged by mass media and deregulated job mediators. Inexhaustible tactics are applied for employees being adept to sagging wages by issuing fragmental information. The dispute on the fiscal hardship had ceased once Abe took the office and the expansionary fiscal policy revived. Therefore, citizens have to make a pause of their restless move and think more deeply to audit the information provided by mass media.

3.   Growth is not imperative. Mass media succeeded in planting the imperativeness of economic growth into the mind of most Japanese. This is based on the myth of the *trickle down*. That is, most Japanese believe that if economy expands as a whole, anyone can share the wealth to some degree. However, the GES is upheld by the presumption of reducing wages, and hence there is no surplus for employees by economic growth. The GES only aggravates the income disparity between employees and employers. Moreover, the GES stands on the assumption that all produced goods are purchased. Nevertheless, since the MPC of employees is thought to be higher than that of employers, the total consumption demand is conversely reduced, and thus the domestic business stagnates against the government's will. Accordingly, economic growth is not imperative for almost all Japanese.

4.   Regaining job diversity. It is an undeniable fact that Japanese firms continue to accumulate huge retained profits during this decade, and that income distribution becomes appallingly disadvantageous for employees. Therefore, it is not unreasonable that employees demand to raise wages. This makes breathing space for various jobs and small business and progresses the job diversity. The widened job diversity will contribute to Japanese economy in the following two senses. First, affluent buffers are created in preparation for the exogenous and unanticipated shocks under the globalization of economies. The industrial structure of advanced economies has become alike by the globalization. This implies that these economies are vulnerable to

macroeconomic shocks such as Lehman shock. One large shock is amplified by the homogeneity of the industrial structure. In contrast, an economy, which possesses various kinds of job, is robust against such a devastating situation. Second, the raised wages heightens the *aggregate* purchasing power of the economy. Although some precautions are necessary in the process of the wage increase, raised wages surely make the breathing space for small business as well. As above discussed, looking back on the Japanese industrial history, one can see that small business can be regarded as an embryo of a future excellent company and/or a key industry. In this sense, regaining the job diversity is one of the most precious legacies for our next generation.

Notes

1 Recently, ECB decided to apply QE (Quantitative Easing) policy to the financial market. Our theory predicts that this will conversely lower the inflation rate against its intension as far as the money has kept its confidence and hyperinflation is not provoked.
2 One must note that even the United States, a key currency country, has given up the extreme QE policy in 2014. Also note that in Japan, which is not a key currency country, there is no guarantee that overseas residents will receive yen without serious discount.
3 See Otaki (2015, Ch. 2) on the dynamic microeconomic foundation for the multiplier process.

References

Burke, E. (2009) *The Reflections on the Revolution in France*, edited by L. G. Mitchell. Oxford World's Classics. [Originally published in 1790]
Hanazaki, M. (2014) *Corporate Governance* (in Japanese). Tokyo: Iwanami-Shoten.
Keynes, J. M. (2013) Economic possibilities for our grandchildren. In *Essays in Persuasion, Collected Writings of John Maynard Keynes*, Vol. 9. Cambridge, UK: Cambridge University Press. [Originally published in 1930]
Otaki, M. (2015) *Keynesian Economics and Price Theory: Re-orientation of a Theory of Monetary Economy.* Tokyo: Springer.

Index